YOU BE THE JUDGE

YOU
BE THE
JUDGE

H. CLARK ADAMS QC

DUNDURN
TORONTO

Editor: Nigel Heseltine
Copy Editor: Britanie Wilson
Design: Courtney Horner
Printer: Webcom

Library and Archives Canada Cataloguing in Publication

Adams, H. Clark
      You be the judge / by H. Clark Adams.

Also issued in electronic formats.
ISBN 978-1-55488-978-5

      I. Title.

PS8601.D4525Y69 2011   C818'.6   C2011-903827-7

1   2   3   4   5   15   14   13   12   11

We acknowledge the support of the **Canada Council for the Arts** and the **Ontario Arts Council** for our publishing program. We also acknowledge the financial support of the **Government of Canada** through the **Canada Book Fund** and **Livres Canada Books**, and the **Government of Ontario** through the **Ontario Book Publishing Tax Credit** and the **Ontario Media Development Corporation**.

Printed and bound in Canada.
www.dundurn.com

Dundurn
3 Church Street, Suite 500
Toronto, Ontario, Canada
M5E 1M2

Gazelle Book Services Limited
White Cross Mills
High Town, Lancaster, England
LA1 4XS

Dundurn
2250 Military Road
Tonawanda, NY
U.S.A. 14150

This book is dedicated to my wife, Jane, who proofread and typed the manuscript, with thanks to my sister, Patricia Boe, who critiqued the English, and my daughter, Lynne, for her computer expertise.

CONTENTS

PART I

THE
CASES

Lynne Smith

vs.

Gerald Brown

Opening Statement

The plaintiff, Lynne Smith, feels she was stood up by her fiancé, the defendant, Gerald Brown, and wishes to recover her monetary loss. Brown, on the other hand, says he was dumped by Smith and wants his ring back.

The Evidence

Lynne Smith and Gerald Brown had known each other as high school friends, but it was not until about five years after graduation that their paths crossed again. They dated for about three years and Gerald proposed marriage to Lynne and gave her a ring, which he said cost him $4,000. The couple set a date some three months away and Lynne went full speed ahead to arrange the wedding. She put a deposit of $400 on a hall for the reception, which could accommodate 200 people. Among her three bridesmaids was Gerald's sister, Susan. The evidence was that Lynne and Susan had not really got along during the courtship, but that Lynne felt some minor obligation to have her included in the wedding party. Gerald was close to his sister and it appears that he pressured Lynne to have Susan included in the wedding party. Almost from the beginning Susan, according to Lynne, wanted to play a major part in the ongoing arrangements and Lynne resented her interference. On several occasions they had major fights over the wedding plans and Gerald invariably took his sister's side. Lynne thought everything would eventually work out with her sister-in-law to be and continued preparation for the wedding ceremony. The material for the wedding dress was purchased at a cost of $700 and a seamstress was hired to make the dress. The seamstress was paid in advance for her estimated time in making the dress, a sum of $350. Flowers were ordered and a deposit paid in the amount of $250. Caterers were selected and a menu decided upon and a further deposit of $10 per person for a total of $2,000 was paid.

Lynne's evidence was that Gerald did not contribute any monies toward the deposits made by her and, in fact, as a result of his recent layoff from his job, borrowed $75 from Lynne for the deposit on his tuxedo.

Lynne testified that about one month before the wedding date, Gerald, without discussion or notice, advised Lynne that he was calling the whole thing off. Lynne believed that Gerald's decision was a result of a dispute she had with Susan over the style of the dresses the bridesmaids would wear.

Susan did not testify.

Gerald is demanding return of the $4,000 ring he gave to Lynne and is denying any obligation he might have for the expenses incurred by Lynne. He did not give any evidence in regard to what Lynne said was his unilateral decision to call off the engagement and wedding, but said that he was entitled to his ring.

The bottom line is that Lynne wishes to be reimbursed her expenses: $700 for the wedding dress and $350 for the seamstress, a $250 deposit for the flowers, $400 for the hall rental deposit, and $2,000 paid to the caterers. She also wants the $75 back she paid for Gerald's tuxedo. Her total claim amounts to $3,775. Gerald wants his ring back.

The question to be decided: whether there was a contract and, if so, was there a breach of contract?

You be the judge.

JAMES KARSTON

VS.

THE PLUMBING PLACE

OPENING STATEMENT

The plaintiff, James Karston, entered into a written contract with the defendant, The Plumbing Place, and paid a deposit. He alleges no work was ever done. The defendant is countersuing for breach of contract and for damages that followed from not being able to complete the contract, suffering, as a result, a loss of potential profit.

THE EVIDENCE

Karston checked out the credentials and experience of The Plumbing Place and determined they had designed and installed bathrooms and showers for 18 years. Karston and The Plumbing Place entered into a contract for the installation of a new shower in the master bedroom in Karston's home. The Plumbing Place attended at Karston's with two designers to determine what was necessary and to give a price. An enclosed shower was already present in a corner of the bedroom. It had two solid outside walls, a solid inside wall in which the water pipes were installed, and another inside wall that had the door to the shower. Karston wanted the new shower to have ceramic tile on the floor and the two outside walls. The inside walls were to be of glass with a glass door.

The designers drew up a plan and gave a price of $7,000. Karston paid a $3,500 deposit.

When the workers came several weeks later with the specially ordered tiles and plumbing supplies, they realized that there was a problem about the installation of the water pipes. Because the new shower's two inside walls were to be glass they realized the water supply pipes would have to be installed in one of the two outside walls. This would create a problem in the winter with the likelihood of the pipes freezing.

The workers phoned their supervisor and he came out to the job site and viewed the situation and advised Karston that the job would cost an additional $500. Karston refused to pay and The Plumbing Place refused to proceed with the work.

After several heated telephone conversations between the parties in which unpleasant remarks were made, matters came to a standstill.

Karston, after several months elapsed with failure to obtain return of his deposit, started the court action. The Plumbing Place commenced a defence and counterclaim saying it was entitled to keep the deposit and sought damages for loss of profit in not being able to complete the job.

During the trial, both parties were a little bit more than nasty to each other and on several occasions I was obliged to advise them that their conduct was unacceptable and if it continued I would adjourn the case to a date at which calmness and politeness would prevail.

The questions to be decided today: whether on the evidence the plaintiff should recover his deposit and whether, as a result of what appears to be a breach of contract, the defendant can obtain monetary damages for his loss of worth?

You be the judge.

JOHN STILLWELL

VS.

LONGSHORE BOARD OF EDUCATION AND JACK SNIDER, PRINCIPAL OF LONG BEACH PUBLIC SCHOOL

OPENING STATEMENT

The plaintiff, John Stillwell, the father of a 12-year-old slightly autistic son attending Long Beach Public School, has requested information in regard to his son Robert's progress. The defendants, Longshore Board of Education (the Board) and Jack Snider, have refused to provide reports on Robert's progress.

THE EVIDENCE

John Stillwell is divorced from his wife, Emma. They have joint custody of Robert. The divorce procedure was a nasty one and Emma has refused to provide any school records for John. The separation agreement provides that both parents shall have joint custody of Robert, but, in fact, Robert has resided with his mother.

At some point several years after the divorce, Emma was unable to look after Robert and John couldn't because he had a job in an isolated community in the far north. The parties attended with their lawyers before the judge who made the original custody order and the custody agreement was revised to give custody of Robert to Earl Stillwell, a brother of John. The custody order in favour of Earl was to be for one year.

The revised custody was filed with Jack Snider, the principal of Robert's school. All reports from the school in regard to Robert were given routinely to Earl.

Jack Snider, the principal, refused to co-operate even though he apparently knew that John was concerned about his son, particularly with his learning ability because of his autism.

John went over Jack Snider's head and wrote letters to the Board superintendent requesting reports on Robert. After four or five letters, the Board wrote to John refusing information on Robert. The Board took the position that only Earl could be provided with the information, notwithstanding that Earl's custody for one year had long since expired.

John then sought legal advice and his lawyer wrote a letter to the Board explaining that the custody in favour of Earl had expired and that John and Emma had joint custody and both were entitled to be informed of Robert's progress.

The Board continued to refuse to provide the information to John, although it was providing the information to Emma.

John then brought this action to force the Board and its principal to co-operate, and he also sought monetary relief for his time and trouble and for his lawyer's fees.

The question here: whether the plaintiff is entitled to the relief he sought, namely to get reports from the defendants on his son's progress?

You be the judge.

Alan and Emily Cherry

vs.

Quick Air

Opening Statement

The plaintiffs, Alan and Emily Cherry, took a flight to Cuba on Quick Air, the defendant, in January 2009. Their flight included 11 days at a nice resort. On arrival in Cuba their luggage could not be found and it included Alan's essential medicine for his heart condition. The Cherrys said their holiday was ruined and they are suing for return of their money paid for the trip.

The Evidence

The Cherrys bought a package deal that included a flight, 11 days at a resort in Varadero, and all their transportation to and from the airport in Cuba. The price for each of them was $1,750.

They had not previously taken a trip by air.

Both Alan and Emily testified that when they checked in at Pearson International in Toronto they were told all their liquid items such as hair shampoo, toothpaste, and Alan's liquid heart medicine, specifically nitroglycerine, had to be packed in their suitcase for checking in and not put in their carry on.

Alan Cherry gave his age as 86 and Emily's as 82.

An airline service representative testified that none of their employees would ever give such erroneous information to anyone.

In any event, when their plane arrived in Cuba the luggage could not be found. All the other passengers had picked up their luggage and departed the air terminal and only the Cherrys remained.

Emily spoke to someone in the terminal who seemed to be in charge of lost luggage and after several more hours the Cherrys were informed that their luggage, for unknown reasons, was still in Toronto but would come on the next flight two days later.

Alan became even more agitated and his need for his nitroglycerine became urgent.

The airline representative from Quick Air told the Cherrys that the flight was returning to Toronto shortly and that there were available seats. Not wanting to be without his medicine Alan Cherry decided to return to Toronto, arriving around 11:30 p.m.

Once in Toronto they tried for three hours to get their luggage, which Alan said was lost in the terminal building.

Finally around 3:00 a.m. their luggage was found and they took a taxi home to Barrie. No public transportation to Barrie was available at 3:00 a.m.

The Cherrys are suing for return of what they paid for the holiday and for the cost for the taxi ride home in the amount of $160 and for their court costs.

Today I have to decide on the evidence if the plaintiffs are entitled to recover as a result of the apparent inability of the defendant to turn over the Cherrys' luggage.

You be the judge.

5

James Snow

vs.

We Park —You Fly

Opening Statement

The plaintiff, James Snow, is suing the defendant, We Park — You Fly, for inconvenience for the loss of his keys on returning to Toronto Airport.

The Evidence

James Snow left his car at the valet parking terminal of We Park — You Fly. The system used by the defendant was that someone wishing to park leaves his vehicle with the keys in the car and gets a quick ride to the airport by shuttle bus. Upon returning to the airport Snow would simply phone the defendant, and upon returning to the parking terminal his car would be ready to go.

Snow was back at the parking lot at about 11:15 p.m., 20 minutes after leaving the airport terminal. He testified that his car was not available and when he enquired about this he was advised that the defendant had not been able to bring his car because the defendant could not locate Snow's keys.

Snow also said his house keys were on the key chain with his car keys as was the only key to his office.

The defendant apparently made many attempts over a period of two hours to find Snow's keys but without success.

The defendant, according to Snow, tried to excuse the problem by saying he couldn't have left the keys when he left his vehicle. They also referred to the clause on the ticket he received when he left his car that the defendant would not be liable for loss or damage to his car.

The defendant eventually said they would get keys made and deliver the car to his home the next day.

Snow was obliged to take a taxi across the city to his home, but on realizing his house key was with his car keys he phoned an all-night locksmith to come and let him in. The locksmith was obliged to install a new lock set at Snow's house and, the next day, at his office.

Snow testified that he incurred a taxi charge of $46, a locksmith charge for his house of $245, it being an after-hours job, and $189 for the new lock at his office. He also indicated that he thought the parking charges for his car should be reimbursed. Those charges amounted to $160 for the time he was away. He also felt he should be reimbursed for his inconvenience and stress.

Snow's car was delivered to his home two days later.

The question to be decided: whether the defendant can avoid liability. To make this determination, as always, I have to weigh the evidence.

You be the judge.

6

Grace Becker

vs.

British American Insurance Co.

Opening Statement

The plaintiff, Grace Becker, is suing the defendant, British American Insurance Co., for loss of her limousine and the defendant is refusing to pay.

The Evidence

Becker had a limo, a car, and a truck, all of which she periodically rented out. The limo was driven by her but she wasn't making much money on it and decided to sell it. She parked it on the lot of a local garage in Guelph with a FOR SALE sign on the windshield. Becker said she got little response to her sign over a period of about five months. She said the only time the vehicle was used was when she took her sister on Sundays to see their parents in Mount Forest.

Becker testified that on Sunday she went to pick up the limo from the lot only to find it had disappeared. She had the only set of keys and was the only person allowed to drive it.

Becker said that on finding the vehicle gone she phoned her husband on her cellphone and he told her to contact the police. Rather than phoning the police with her cellphone, she returned home and phoned from there.

Police came to her home and took a report and told Grace that they would let her know if and when they found her limo.

On Monday morning she received a telephone call from the police who found her car in a parking lot in an industrial area of Kitchener. She drove over to Kitchener and met the police who took her to the lot where her locked limo was totally burned out.

She filed a claim with the defendant insurance company for $20,000, although at trial she agreed on cross-examination that the limo was old and probably not worth more than $8,000.

The insurance company denied her claim and on that basis she commenced this court case for $20,000.

On cross-examination Grace admitted she was the sole possessor of the keys to the vehicle. She also admitted that she had a part-time job at a printing plant in close proximity to the place where her car was found. The defendant's representatives questioned her on the use of her cellphone to call her husband but then they produced telephone records from the phone company that proved she had not, on the day in question, phoned her husband.

The defendant called an expert witness, Roy Phelps, to give evidence about the vehicle. He was a specialist in steering columns and said that he did a thorough analysis of the vehicle's steering column and that there was no way the vehicle could be started without the keys.

A police witness testified that there was no evidence of glass at the garage where she tried to sell her car and he concluded that no one broke into the car to steal it.

I have to decide, based on the testimony, if the plaintiff is entitled to be paid by the defendant insurance company or whether there is sufficient evidence for them to avoid payment.

You be the judge.

7

RALPH NIZER

VS.

LONG RANGE TRANSPORT LTD.

OPENING STATEMENT

The plaintiff, Ralph Nizer, was a driver for the defendant company, Long Range Transport Ltd., and is suing for unpaid wages and the defendant is counterclaiming for its expenses in retrieving its truck to Hamilton, Ontario.

THE EVIDENCE

Nizer was hired as a driver of a transport to haul various goods to Atlanta, Georgia, and to pick up goods on his way back to Hamilton, Ontario. He was to receive 40 cents per mile plus $20 per hour waiting time at delivery and pick up points, as well as waiting time at the border. He was on probation for a period of four months.

This lawsuit arises out of a trip from Hamilton to Atlanta. Nizer had to wait three hours at the border for clearance and this is one of the items for which he seeks payment. On his second day after his final delivery in Atlanta he noticed that his fuel gauge was showing one-quarter full and he pulled into a truck centre where he decided he would spend the night. He called his dispatcher in Hamilton and requested permission to obtain fuel, but was refused by the dispatcher.

The evidence of the company, represented by John Charles, was that the company had an arrangement with certain stations where they received a sizable discount on the fuel charges and the station where Nizer was parked was not one of them. Charles also stated that while Nizer had a credit card it had to be activated by the company before he could obtain fuel.

According to Charles, the company had a monitoring system so that it knew at any time where the truck was located and how much fuel the driver had at his disposal. Charles said Nizer had sufficient fuel to get back to at least Buffalo where the company had a discount supplier.

Nizer phoned the next morning and again requested permission to fill up. He was again refused and was told to proceed to Buffalo.

Nizer testified that he was extremely nervous about proceeding as he would be primarily on freeways and didn't want to get stuck as he put it "in the middle of nowhere."

The plaintiff did drive another 300 miles and testified his fuel tank gauge was showing almost empty. He stopped at another service centre about 100 miles from Buffalo and again phoned his dispatcher and again was refused a fill-up. He then said he told the dispatcher where he was and said he was abandoning the rig and making his way home. He then proceeded to call his daughter to come and pick him up.

Charles testified that the company then drove another driver to the location and drove the truck home to Hamilton without the necessity of obtaining more fuel. The company did not produce the driver to prove the allegations about driving back to Hamilton without a fill-up.

The questions here: whether the company was justified in taking the position they did and whether the plaintiff was justified in his position?

You be the judge.

8

See Thru Windows Inc.

vs.

Jason Stowkowski

Opening Statement

The plaintiff, See Thru Windows Inc., is suing the defendant, Jason Stowkowski, for doors and windows ordered by the defendant for his house and the defendant has a counterclaim for return of his deposit.

The Evidence

Jason Stowkowski, after receiving a quotation from See Thru Windows for new windows and doors for his house, entered into a written contract for $18,500. He paid a deposit of $8,500. The balance was to be paid on installation. The plaintiff spent approximately one day at the defendant's house measuring the openings for the replacement doors and windows. The plaintiff was a supplier of windows but not the manufacturer.

The company said it would take about six weeks to have everything made. In fact it took about 12 weeks and the plaintiff only admitted after many telephone calls from Stowkowski that the windows had arrived and would be installed in about three weeks.

When talking to the defendant, the plaintiff said that since the order took so long to fill, the price from the manufacturer had increased and they would require a further deposit of $2,000.

They indicated they would not proceed without the additional payment.

Stowkowski refused to pay and the plaintiff brought this action for payment.

The question here is simply this: was there a valid enforceable contract and, if so, was there a breach of contract and, if so, by whom?

You be the judge.

— 9 —

CHARLES WILSON
VS.
SNELGRASS DEVELOPMENT LTD.

OPENING STATEMENT

Charles Wilson is suing Snelgrass Developments Ltd. for an abatement in the purchase price of a lot that he alleges was misdescribed on the company's brochure.

THE EVIDENCE

Snelgrass is the developer of an exclusive high-priced subdivision in Mississauga, Ontario.

Wilson and his wife looked at this subdivision along with several others but liked the look of the Snelgrass lots. In particular they liked a ravine lot at the bend in Walnut Street. This particular lot because of its location in the inside curve of the road had a smaller frontage of 50 feet, but a considerable depth and a rear dimension of 175 feet.

The lawsuit centres around the lot dimensions. The lot was undeveloped as were adjacent lots in both directions for six or seven lots. The lot was staked with survey stakes and it was clearly evident what Wilson was interested in.

Snelgrass's brochure had a sketch of the survey, which showed the measurements of all four sides of the lot. The subject matter of this dispute was the easterly limit of the lot, which showed on the sketch of survey as being 310 feet from the road. The westerly limit of the lot indicated a length of 180 feet.

Wilson put in an offer to purchase that described the lot as being lot 33 on plan 2160. The offer to purchase was for $750,000 with a deposit of $25,000, and was to close on or about four months after acceptance by Snelgrass. On the lot was to be built a rather nice two-storey house of about 4,000 square feet and a three-car garage.

Snelgrass, within a few days of accepting the offer, had a surveyor come in and plot the location of the foundation and in the process the surveyor put in stakes marking the building location, as well as stakes marking the sides of the lot. When the stakes were all in place, the surveyor prepared a sketch and the sketch indicated that the length of the easterly limit was 210 feet.

When Wilson was presented with the sketch for his approval, he immediately contacted Snelgrass and demanded a reduction of $25,000 off the purchase price.

Snelgrass testified that they refused his request for an abatement and explained that the original sketch in its brochure was a typographical error and that the easterly lot limit was actually 210 feet and not 310 feet. They also pointed out the two lots to the east of lot 33 had depths similar to the surveyor's sketch.

Wilson, on cross-examination by the lawyer for Snelgrass, admitted that he viewed the lot and knew he was getting the area that he expected, but he was not satisfied with the lot dimensions.

The question to be answered: whether Wilson, being satisfied with the area, can use an incorrect dimension to obtain a reduced price?

You be the judge.

SANDRA STRONG

VS.

EMPIRE DISCOUNT FURNITURE

OPENING STATEMENT

The plaintiff, Sandra Strong, is suing the defendant, Empire Discount Furniture, for breach of contract regarding a special order for living room furniture.

THE EVIDENCE

Strong testified that she recently moved into a new condominium and wanted some furniture for her living room. She looked at furniture at several stores and finally found what she thought would be right for her at Empire Discount Furniture.

She indicated that the design was good but that the furniture on display in the showroom was not satisfactory. The salesperson, along with the store manager, showed her a number of fabrics and she settled on one. The furniture had to be made by the manufacturer and Empire told Sandra that it would take about eight to nine weeks to be delivered to the store.

Sandra paid a deposit of $700 for the furniture, a couch and love seat, which had a total cost of $4,580.

Sandra was pleased when in six weeks' time she had a call on her answering service from the store advising her that the furniture was in and could be delivered the next day.

Sandra phoned the store and talked to Sam, who was her salesperson, and advised him that she would be at work for the next two days, but that her son, Daren, who was 13, would be at home and would let the delivery persons in. She prepared a cheque and left it with her son to give to the driver. Sam was happy with this arrangement.

The next day the furniture was delivered and Daren handed over the cheque for $3,880.

When Sandra arrived home, she was astounded and upset to find that the material used on the furniture was not what she had ordered. She immediately phoned Sam and he denied it was the wrong material. After several phone calls to Empire and several letters brought no results, Sandra brought this action.

It appears that the parties agreed to mediation of this dispute and during mediation Empire agreed to settle on the basis of giving Sandra a refund of $350. Sandra refused.

During the trial, Sandra brought in one of the cushions from the love seat and a swatch of the material that was supposed to be used. Empire testified that the swatch was not from its samples, but on cross-examination by Sandra's lawyer admitted that they could have been mistaken.

Sandra wants her money back and agrees to have Empire pick up the furniture.

Was there a breach of contract?

You be the judge.

11

Jennifer Hurdle

vs.

Jeffrey Capriotti

Opening Statement

The plaintiff, Jennifer Hurdle, is suing the defendant, Jeffrey Capriotti, for injuries she sustained during what she alleges was an attack by Capriotti's dog, Tyler.

The Evidence

The plaintiff was walking along Ironwood Court after walking her two children to school. Jeffrey Capriotti lives about a block away from Jennifer and is the owner of a six-year-old Newfoundland dog.

Jennifer testified that the neighbours all knew about Tyler, and that for the most part Tyler was confined to the defendant's yard. She indicated that there is a gate in the fence at the side of Capriotti's house where Tyler is taken in and out of the house. There is a sign on the gate, BEWARE OF DOG.

On the day in question just as Jennifer was passing Capriotti's house, she heard a loud bark and stopped. Tyler bounded out of the gate and ran toward Jennifer. The plaintiff admitted she was terrified of dogs and moved off the sidewalk and onto the edge of the road.

Jennifer testified that as Tyler approached her, Jeffrey came running out of the house yelling at Tyler to come back. Tyler didn't stop and bounded up to Jennifer, knocking her to the pavement. As a result, she hit her face on the curb, sustaining severe facial injuries that subsequently required surgery by a plastic surgeon.

The defendant said that Jennifer overreacted and when she saw Tyler she fell off the sidewalk, onto the road, and hit her arm on the curb. He also said that Jennifer was known to be overreactive to dogs and that Tyler did stop when called.

The question I have to decide: whether Jennifer's injuries were caused by the dog knocking her over or whether she lost control and fell off the sidewalk?

You be the judge.

12

BULK HAY LTD.

VS.

GERALD NASH

OPENING STATEMENT

The plaintiff, Bulk Hay Ltd., is suing the defendant, Gerald Nash, for the cost of hay purchased from Nash and the resulting loss of profit they suffered in not being able to resell it as mushroom hay.

THE EVIDENCE

Nash is a farmer on the 7th concession of Adjala Township in Simcoe County, where he has farmed for 20 years.

Across the road from Nash's farm is a farm owned by Craig Sawyer. Sawyer was a widower in his 80th year. When he could no longer work his farm, he moved into town to a retirement home and rented his land to Nash.

Nash used the Sawyer farm primarily for hay and had a reputation for producing good crops. The crops were to some extent of a superior quality partly because of Nash's farming technique and partly because of the excellent soil.

After several years of renting Sawyer's land, Nash bought the farm in 2001 but left the house empty, as he lived directly across the 7th line. The house was an old farm house, which Sawyer had not maintained while living in it and which continued to fall apart after Sawyer moved into town.

In 2001 the owner of Bulk Hay, James Swanson, was searching for hay for his hay business and drove by the old Sawyer farm where Nash had piled up a row of huge round bales of hay. Nash testified that he believed there were upwards of 90 bales piled two deep along the driveway, some 30 to 40 feet from the abandoned house.

In October, 2001, Bulk Hay made a deal to purchase 30 of these bales at the price of $100 per bale. Nash was paid by cheque and agreed to allow Bulk Hay until the spring of 2002 to remove the bales.

In the fall of 2002 the bales were still on site and Nash phoned on several occasions requesting Bulk Hay to remove the bales. He explained that the house has been taken over by rats and that they were into the hay bales as well. Bulk Hay requested a further extension for the pick up of the bales until the spring of 2003. Nash agreed but reiterated his concern that their hay was deteriorating in quality and was becoming infected with mice and rats.

By June 7, 2003, it became obvious to Nash that he would have to insist on removal of the hay and he gave Bulk Hay until September 30 to do so. In fact, on June 29, he sent a letter to Bulk Hay, at their office in Alliston, demanding removal.

September 30 came and went and the hay was still on the lane. The bales were disintegrating and Nash decided to take action. He sold 67 of the bales to a neighbour for bedding at the neighbour's horse farm.

By June 7, 2004, the bales were falling apart and were no longer of any use so Nash took his front end loader and put the bales in his hay wagon and dumped them at the back of his farm. He testified that he made about 30 trips to the back of the farm.

In early July, James Swanson of Bulk Hay was driving by and noticed the hay was all gone. He approached Nash who told him the hay was still available, but he would have to load it up at the back of the farm.

Words were exchanged and Swanson left saying he would see his lawyer and would be suing Nash.

Swanson testified that the hay had been resold by him to a company in New York State to be used as mushroom hay. He said the New York company was upset that it couldn't be delivered and they indicated they would no longer do business with Bulk Hay.

Swanson said that because of the deterioration of the hay the agricultural authorities would not let it be transported across into New York.

As a result Swanson said he lost $4,000 profit.

When cross-examined by Nash's lawyer, Swanson said that the hay was left from the fall of 2001 until 2003 so that it would partially decompose. The buyers of mushroom hay wanted partially rotten hay.

He also testified that there was no time limit on removal of the hay from Nash's farm.

Also, he added that he lost future business with his New York customers, which he blamed on Nash.

The question to be decided: whether Nash is responsible for the loss suffered by Bulk Hay and for the loss of the purchased hay that Nash dumped at the back of his farm?

You be the judge.

13

TIM AND LAURA O'GRADY

VS.

GEORGE AND SYLVIA WATERS

OPENING STATEMENT

The plaintiffs, Tim and Laura O'Grady, as purchasers of a house at 189 Strong Avenue in Brampton, are suing the defendants, George and Sylvia Waters, as vendors of the house, for the cost of fixing a swimming pool that was to have been in operating condition on the closing of the transaction.

THE EVIDENCE

The O'Gradys through a real estate agent agreed to purchase the home of the Waters at 189 Strong Avenue in Brampton. Tim O'Grady produced the agreement of purchase and sale dated March 10, 2008. The agreement contained a clause to the effect that the pool and pool equipment were in working condition and would be at the time the deal closed on April 15, 2008.

When the O'Gradys saw the house, there was about a foot of snow and the pool and pool cover were almost totally covered.

When the O'Gradys finally had possession of the property on April 15, they took immediate steps to put the pool into working order. As they had no previous experience in preparing a pool for the summer, they called in a pool company to open the pool.

Jack Snell of Glorious Pools testified on behalf of the O'Gradys that the pool liner was ripped and would have to be replaced at a cost of $3,750. He also said the pool filter would have to be replaced at a cost estimated at $3,400. The heater had not been drained in the fall and the heat exchanger was cracked and leaking and would have to be replaced at a further cost of $1,700.

The O'Gradys were somewhat skeptical about this report and called in Bill White of Leisure Pools to check things out. White came in with virtually the same report as Snell, but with a price that was $1,200 higher than Snell's.

With Glorious Pools back on the scene, Jack Snell informed the O'Gradys that a municipal permit would have to be obtained for the work to be done. An application for work to be done was prepared by Snell and submitted to the proper authorities at Brampton City Hall.

Within two days of receipt of the application Terry Onschuk of the bylaw office attended at the O'Grady property. He advised the plaintiffs that, following complaints from neighbours the summer before, he had inspected the pool and found the ripped liner and two or three inches of algae growing in the pool. He said in testimony that the pool was giving off a strong odour and this is what the neighbours were complaining about.

He advised that the pool be closed down unless the owners fixed the problem within two weeks. No follow up was made by the municipality.

The defendants testified that they had used the pool regularly the previous summer and denied any knowledge of mechanical problems in the filter and heater.

The lawyer representing Waters raised as a defence the legal defence "buyer beware," and indicated that the purchasers had an opportunity to inspect the property before closing.

The lawyer representing the O'Gradys relied on the clause in the agreement that the pool and equipment would be in good working order on closing.

The question to be decided: whether the defence of "buyer beware" or the plaintiff's allegation that they relied on the clause in the agreement should decide the case?

You be the judge.

14

Sylvia Heron

vs.

Owen Sound Concrete Driveway Paving Ltd.

Opening Statement

The plaintiff, Sylvia Heron, is suing the defendant, Owen Sound Concrete Driveway Paving Ltd., for the cost of replacing her driveway, which she alleges was improperly installed by the defendant.

The Evidence

Heron purchased a newly built house three years before this action was started. Up until she contracted with the defendant to pave her driveway, she had a gravel drive. She testified that she was advised to wait two or three years for the driveway base to settle before having it paved.

In July of 2004 she got three estimates and selected Owen Sound Concrete Driveway Paving. The contract drawn up by Owen Sound manager, Leslie Jones, specified that the driveway would be 20 feet wide by 65 feet long and would have pre-cast concrete edges or curbs that would be three inches above the level of the paved surface.

The cost of the concrete driveway and edges and base

materials and labour was to be $7,350. The driveway was warranted for six months.

The work was commenced by the defendant and completed in two weeks. The defendant brought in a roller to compact the sand and gravel base and the concrete edges were installed by the end of August, 2004.

In April of 2005, Heron noticed that there were thin layers of concrete coming off the cement driveway and by June 7, 2005, even larger pieces about one-sixteenth of an inch were peeling off in various locations.

The plaintiff called Leslie Jones and complained about the problem and he said that he didn't know why this was happening, but in any event the warranty had expired.

Jones did, however, agree to look at the problem and when he viewed the driveway said it looked like it had been damaged by salt during the winter.

Heron testified that she did not put salt on the driveway and when she was out with her car she did not park in the drive but went into the garage immediately.

Jones's second theory was that there must have been something defective in the concrete that he used on the job. The concrete was purchased from York Ready-Mix Concrete, a local supplier.

Jones called, as a witness, Sam Biltmore from York Ready-Mix Concrete. Biltmore said that they had used the same material for mixing concrete for 18 years and had no problems.

The questions to be decided: who is responsible for the problems being encountered by Sylvia Heron and, if the defendant is responsible, can the warranty clause be used to let the company escape liability?

You be the judge.

15

STAR MOVERS LTD.

VS.

STANLEY BAIRD

OPENING STATEMENT

The plaintiff, Star Movers Ltd., is suing the defendant, Stanley Baird, for the cost of moving his household contents. Baird has refused to pay.

THE EVIDENCE

The plaintiff, at the request of the defendant, gave an estimate for moving the defendant's household contents from 350 Douglas Street in Guelph to Tindle Street, a distance of about three miles.

When Marcel Stormont, the plaintiff's estimator, went to Baird's home he was shown the items to be moved. He was also advised by Baird that his dining room table was an Austrian antique with a marble top that Baird suggested should be crated but he wasn't sure.

Stormont admired the beautiful table and agreed that to guard against mishaps, which in all likelihood would not be covered by insurance, it would be a good idea to crate the table.

Based on the usual charges for the rest of the household contents and the crating of the table and the time involved, including the three mile trip, Star Movers gave an estimate of $1,200. Baird signed the estimate and a moving date of June 27 was scheduled. Star measured the table so that they could have a crate prepared for the moving day.

On June 27, Star Movers with a crew of three men arrived at 350 Douglas Street at around 7:30 a.m. They received no answer when they knocked at both the front and side doors. Jack Snow, the truck driver, who was also the crew supervisor, tried calling Baird. There was no answer. Then he called Baird's cellphone number and Baird answered. He told Snow he had an emergency call from the hospital where he still was, but said he would be home in 45 minutes.

The moving crew decided to leave and have a coffee at a nearby doughnut shop. On returning to Baird's house they found him not to be there and they waited another half-hour before Baird arrived. In the meantime they installed their ramp to the front door and unloaded the crate, which they placed on the front lawn.

The first thing Baird said when he arrived, not apologizing for his tardiness, was that he decided he didn't need the crate for his table. Snow told him very politely that the cost had been figured into the estimate. Baird replied that he expected the cost to be removed from the bill.

It took about three hours for the contents to be placed in the truck including the crated dining room table.

Led by Baird the truck arrived at Tindle Street. The occupants of the Tindle Street house were in the course of moving out and had much of their furniture on the lawn and in the garage, and their moving truck was blocking the entrance so that Star Movers could not get close to the front door.

Baird talked to the owner and was advised that they needed at least another hour to get all their stuff out.

Baird spoke to Snow and said he was not prepared to

have Star Movers sit on the street and asked if they had storage facilities. He also mumbled something about having the house painted before he moved in.

Snow phoned his office and was told they had room to store the truck load. The cost of storage would be $125 per day plus unloading and reloading. Baird agreed to have his furniture stored and the truck with crew proceeded to the storage facility located in the opposite end of the city.

In five days Baird phoned Star and said he had access to the house and would like his stuff to be delivered. All of Star's trucks were tied up but they agreed to deliver everything mid-afternoon in two days.

The move took place as agreed and Baird was presented with a bill that included the original $1,200, plus the seven days storage charge of $875, plus four extra hours for travel and unloading and reloading at the storage facility at a cost of $800.

Baird promptly and without any fuss gave Star Movers a cheque for $2,875.

One week later Star Movers received notification from its bank that Baird had issued a stop payment on the cheque.

Phone calls to Baird went unanswered as did a lawyer's letter that Star Movers sent to Baird threatening action.

In his testimony Baird, first, advised the court that he was a lawyer and knew the law. He said the plaintiff was bound by the estimate of $1,200 and he didn't intend to pay more.

In fact, he said, the crate was unnecessary and he thought its cost should be deducted but he wouldn't make a big deal of it.

On cross-examination Baird said he didn't request the storage, but only suggested it because Star Movers couldn't get access to the Tindle Street house and he thought by storing the furniture it would stop the clock from running. He also denied saying anything about painting the house.

The main witness for Star Movers was Snow and he said that the estimate was just that, only an estimate, and that his company never knew exactly how much time would be needed to complete a move or what other problems might arise — such as gaining access to the house on Tindle.

Baird said during his testimony that he was prepared to end the matter today by writing a cheque for $1,200.

The question to be decided: whether an estimate is only an estimate or whether there was a binding contract obligating Baird to pay and Star Movers to accept the $1,200?

You be the judge.

16

JACK STARR

VS.

WHITE CONDOMINIUM CORPORATION

OPENING STATEMENT

The plaintiff, Jack Starr, is suing the defendant, White Condominium Corporation, for damages to his condo caused by a water leak from the condo above. This is a claim by the plaintiff, Jack Starr, at the insistence of Starr's insurance company.

THE EVIDENCE

Starr is the owner of a 1,600-square-foot, two-bedroom condo in the building owned by White Condominium Corporation.

In mid November, 2007, Starr returned from a short trip to Florida to find his condo totally soaked with water. His living room furniture was damaged. Wallpaper in the living room and one wall of the bedroom was hanging pretty much off the walls.

An Emily Carr painting called "Stumps on the Beach" was curled up and, he said, was a mess. The Carr painting was a watercolour on paper valued at $350,000.

The broadloom carpets were drenched.

Starr testified that his insurance company agreed to pay for all damages except to the Carr painting, which was not covered under his homeowner's policy. He received an estimate from a painting restoration expert in Toronto of $7,000 to put the painting back in reasonable condition, but that its value would be greatly diminished.

Starr's insurer, Knox Canada Ltd., through Starr as plaintiff, is claiming $2,750 for cleaning up the apartment furniture and walls.

Starr on his behalf is claiming $7,000 for the restoration of the Carr painting.

The building superintendent, May August, testified that she discovered the water damage when she noticed water leaking out under the condo door, two days after Starr had left for Florida. She immediately went to condo 1710, which was directly above the plaintiff's condo, and found that the owner was at work. The unit's bathroom taps had been left on, the bathtub was overflowing, the bathroom was flooding, and water was running all over the floors in condo 1710.

She shut the taps off and called the owner of 1710 at work. May was successful in talking to the owner who came home and advised May that she had been preparing to have a bath, but received a call saying that her father had been rushed to hospital, so she left in a hurry, forgetting about the bathtub.

The lawyer for White Condominium Corporation called the president, James Walter, as a witness. He testified that the condo corporation was not responsible for what happens in individual apartments but only for the outside walls and common areas. He said in no uncertain terms that Starr had sued the wrong persons.

The question to be decided: whether White Condo Corporation is responsible for the damage?

You be the judge.

17

Bank of Toronto

vs.

Gary Simpson

Opening Statement

The plaintiff, Bank of Toronto, is suing the defendant, Gary Simpson, for monies owing on a credit card account.

The Evidence

George Simpson, the father of Gary, applied for and received a credit card from the plaintiff. George signed a consent form that basically said that Gary could sign for purchases.

Over a period of several years from roughly July, 2005, to June, 2007, while Gary was in his first and second years at the University of Guelph, Gary made purchases of books and other miscellaneous items and charged these to the credit card. George always paid for these and up until July, 2007, the account was in good standing.

At the end of his second year at the University of Guelph, Gary decided to do some extensive travelling throughout Europe and the major portion of his expenses was charged to the credit card. The balance owing as of July, 2008, was $8,363.20.

George Simpson died in early July, 2008, and according to the bank had no estate and the $8,363.20 was uncollectible from his estate.

The bank then decided to pursue Gary for the monies owing and they produced statements as to the expenses incurred by Gary.

In his testimony Gary did not deny the expenses, but he claimed he never signed anything with the bank agreeing to pay.

The bank said they thought Gary had signed as guarantor on the credit card application but were unable to put their hands on the form Gary allegedly signed.

The question to be decided: whether Gary is responsible for the balance owing?

You be the judge.

18

SARAH SMART

VS.

VORTEX LTD.

OPENING STATEMENT

The plaintiff, Sarah Smart, is suing the defendant, Vortex Ltd., for $10,000 for wrongful dismissal. The defence is that Smart was dismissed for cause and is entitled to nothing.

THE EVIDENCE

Sarah Smart was hired by Vortex after the company received her resumé and interviewed her.

The position was that of a receptionist, which involved answering the phone, greeting the public, doing reports and letters on the computer, and making coffee and tea for morning and afternoon breaks for about 10 supervisors and department heads.

Her salary as agreed was $30,000 a year, payable biweekly. The defendant, represented by John Field, the person in charge of the human resources department, testified that the interview went well. He said it was made quite clear to Sarah that she would be on probation for four months to see how things went.

Field said that Sarah came to the interview dressed appropriately but that on her second day on the job, she appeared with torn jeans and an extremely low-cut blouse, which, he pointed out, was similar to the one she is wearing today in court.

Field said he suggested to her that she wear something a little more appropriate for an office and she did turn up on day three in a smart business suit. He said she dressed nicely and conservatively for about three more weeks, but then reverted to extremely low-cut blouses. He said this was a distraction to the employees, predominately male, in the office.

He also said that Sarah chewed gum "furiously," and she was also told about this.

Her typing skills and use of the computer, according to Field, left a great deal to be desired.

One day after Sarah had been working for about three weeks, Field said he was passing through the reception area and Sarah was telling a customer that if he didn't like doing business with Vortex, he could take his business elsewhere.

After work that day, Field and one of the vice-presidents, John Baker, called Sarah in for a talk. Baker testified that Sarah was crying from the start of the interview, but very defiant about suggestions that her dress and attitude were not up to company standards. He said he told Sarah that she would have two weeks to "get with it" or she would be terminated.

At the end of four weeks, Field talked to John Blake and brought him up to date about Sarah's skills, her dress, and her attitude, and on the same day Sarah was handed a letter advising her that she was dismissed.

In her testimony Sarah said there was no reason for her dismissal. She said she was misled by John Field about her responsibilities.

When questioned by the solicitor for Vortex about her inappropriate dress, she replied that she knew Field and several other of the male executives enjoyed standing at the reception counter and looking down the front of her blouse.

Sarah's case was, as the lawyer stated, based on wrongful dismissal.

Vortex's defence was that of just cause after warnings to her.

The question to be determined: whether Sarah was wrongfully dismissed or dismissed for cause?

You be the judge.

19

VENTURE TELEPHONE INC.

VS.

JOSH PERRY

OPENING STATEMENT

The plaintiff, Venture Telephone, is suing the defendant, Josh Perry, for $4,373 for telephone services that the company says have been billed but have not been paid.

THE EVIDENCE

Josh Perry is a self-employed businessman who operates a boat appraisal and surveyor operation in two locations: one office is in Collingwood, Ontario, and the other is in Port Dover, Ontario.

For about five years Perry had been using the services of Venture, which supplied him with regular phones in both his offices and with cellular service.

Perry testified that he spent on the average three days a week in Collingwood and two days in Port Dover. Because of the considerable distance between the two offices, he was on the road a lot and his cost for his cellular service was considerable.

Venture Telephone, represented by an employee named Valerio Goodfellow, gave evidence of the history of Perry's account with the company.

Goodfellow was an excellent witness who had all her facts and figures at her fingertips and explained the accounts clearly and succinctly.

According to her testimony the defendant kept his account in good standing for about five years, but then started falling into arrears.

Sometime around the end of the five years, Perry said, he started to be hassled by the plaintiff, so he started looking for another company for his telephone needs.

Perry said he found an alternate supplier and phoned Venture and said he wished to cancel his phone in area code 705, which was his Collingwood office. He said he believed that cancellation of one phone would automatically cancel his cell and Port Dover phones. He believed this, he said, because Venture sent him only one bill for all its services.

Perry testified that he continued to receive bills from Venture, but thought they were just a mistake and threw them in the garbage.

Goodfellow said that Perry continued to regularly use his Port Dover phone and his cellphone.

When I asked her why Venture waited for two years to commence action, she said that many businesses get behind in their payments and Venture tries to be lenient and also it doesn't want to lose a customer by being nasty.

When Goodfellow cross-examined the defendant as to why he paid his new supplier considerably less than he was paying Venture for the same services, he said he never paid any attention to his bills, but merely handed them to his bookkeeper to pay them.

Perry said he honestly believed that when he contacted Venture to cancel its service that all services would be cancelled.

On cross-examination he said he couldn't remember exactly what he said when he cancelled his phone, but he believed he cancelled the whole contract with Venture.

The question to be answered here: did Perry cancel his whole arrangement with Venture and, if he didn't, is Venture entitled to the $4,373 it claims?

You be the judge.

20

GERRY LISANTI

VS.

PEOPLE'S INSURANCE CO.

OPENING STATEMENT

The plaintiff, Gerry Lisanti, is suing the defendant, his insurance company, People's Insurance Co., for $7,933 for damages to his vehicle. The company has refused to pay.

THE EVIDENCE

Lisanti has had his car insurance with People's for over five years. His policy coverage was from March 12 for one year and had not been changed for five years.

Lisanti saw an advertisement in the *Orangeville Banner* suggesting that persons requiring insurance contact a certain website for a quote from three companies. This was in early January 2008.

He got on his computer and found the site and filled in information about his vehicle, his age, driving record, et cetera, and within a few minutes had quotations from three different insurance brokers. All the quotes were for less than he was paying People's.

As People's had sent him a form to complete before his renewal date of March 12, he wrote on the form that he would be cancelling and going with another company. On the form, a copy of which he introduced into evidence, he said, "I no longer will be insuring with you."

He testified he sent the form to People's by mail on January 27, 2008.

When cross-examined by the lawyer for People's, he was asked why he would have a copy of the form he sent. He replied that he did it because he didn't trust or like insurance companies.

On February 12 while driving his son to the local arena for a hockey practice he skidded on the icy road and hit a hydro pole, causing $5,953 damage to his car and $2,000 to the hydro pole, which had to be replaced.

He called the police but no one was hurt and no charges were laid. The police reported the accident to the local hydro office.

The next step in this scenario was that Gerry Lisanti obtained from his insurance agent a claim form to be filed with the insurer. This form was completed and left with the agent.

About 10 days later the agent phoned Gerry and said his insurance had been cancelled. Gerry rushed down to the agent's office and the agent explained to him that he had advised the insurer to cancel. The agent did not have Gerry's form sent on January 27, 2008, but only a fax from People's saying, "Policy cancelled by insured no further action required."

Over the next few weeks Gerry tried to get to the bottom of this problem, but the insurance company ignored his phone calls and letters.

In desperation Gerry started this action after the hydro people threatened legal action.

The defendant's only witness, Guy Lachance, testified that it received Jerry's form on January 30, 2008 and immediately cancelled the policy. He said Gerry would, in due course, be receiving a rebate of part of the premium for the period January 30 to March 12.

Gerry produced a signed and accepted application for vehicle insurance with his new company effective March 12, 2008.

The questions to be decided: Did Gerry cancel the policy as of January 27, 2008, or did he remain insured at the time of the accident on February 12, 2008? Was the insurance company justified in cancelling the plaintiff's insurance effective January 30, 2008, or did they misinterpret the renewal form on which Lisanti endorsed his intention to cancel?

You be the judge.

Maria Selfridge

vs.

Wedding Time Banquet Hall

Opening Statement

The plaintiff, Maria Selfridge, is suing the defendant, Wedding Time Banquet Hall, for deposit monies paid for a reception to be held following her wedding.

The Evidence

Eight months before she was to be married to her fiancé, James Arnif, Maria and her mother started looking for a hall for the reception. They priced out six halls and settled on the defendant's. The rental for the hall was set at $800 and the meals at $60 per plate. Maria was to advise Joe, the manager, at least one month before the wedding as to the number of guests.

Maria paid a deposit of $200 to hold the hall and a contract was signed. Maria said she told Joe that she could come in and decorate the afternoon before the wedding unless he received a booking for the evening before. Otherwise she would have to decorate on the morning of her wedding.

About five weeks before the wedding date, Maria phoned the hall intending to advise Joe of the number of guests.

No one answered but she recognized Joe's voice on the answering machine. Maria left a message for Joe to call her.

After receiving no reply from Joe for several days, Maria phoned again and continued phoning, according to her testimony, for one week. Each time there was a recorded message and a request to leave a message.

The plaintiff was getting a bit upset and she and her fiancé drove to the hall. To her surprise and horror there was a sign on the door on the letterhead of a trustee in bankruptcy to the effect that the defendant had gone into bankruptcy. She phoned the trustee who told her that she certainly wouldn't be able to use the hall and that he would send her details of the bankruptcy.

Having heard nothing further she commenced this action to recover her deposit. Her claim was served by mail on the defendant's company.

Maria heard nothing more and, with no defence being filed, she requested the court office to put the case on the court list for an assessment. That is what we are dealing with today. An assessment hearing is arranged when the plaintiff files a claim but no defence is filed. At the hearing the plaintiff gives evidence proving her claim.

At the conclusion of her evidence I asked Maria if there was anything else she wished to say and she said she received yesterday a form from the trustee confirming the bankruptcy.

The matter to be decided: whether, in view of the bankruptcy, Maria can collect through this court?

You be the judge.

MARIO PESTRELLI

VS.

CONAIR INC.

OPENING STATEMENT

The plaintiff, Mario Pestrelli, is suing the defendant, Conair Inc., for damages as a result of lost luggage.

THE EVIDENCE

The plaintiff booked a flight to Italy with Conair Inc.

Mario testified that he believed Conair was a discount charter company with rates that were about half what a regular airline would charge. His flight was to leave Toronto and stop in Lisbon, Portugal, where he would switch to another plane and fly on to Milan, Italy. Because of the plane switch he was told at the check-in counter in Toronto that he would have to retrieve his luggage in Lisbon and check-in again for the second leg of his journey to Milan.

He had about 90 minutes between flights in Lisbon.

Mario looked for his luggage in Lisbon and, when it hadn't appeared on the conveyor in about 45 minutes, he talked to the service representative of Conair, who took the information and entered it on her computer. She said she didn't know why he was told to retrieve his luggage — six suitcases — because the normal procedure was to book it straight through and it appeared from her computer that it had, in fact, been booked to Milan.

Mario added that he had so many suitcases because he was to be married in Milan five days after arrival and that he had all his wedding clothes as well as enough clothes for his planned two-month stay in Italy where he was to honeymoon and visit many of his relatives and his fiancée's relatives.

On arrival in Milan he couldn't find his luggage and filed the usual request for a trace with a representative for Conair. Conair explained that there might have been a mix-up in Lisbon, but the company was sure his luggage would arrive and it would, at its expense, deliver it to his hotel in Milan.

Two days after his arrival there was still no luggage and Mario was getting, as he put it, "frantic." It was only three days until his wedding and he had no clothes. He said his beard was growing fast and his fiancée was "freaking out."

On the third day, with no positive report from Conair, Mario went out and bought clothes costing $2,123 and arranged to rent a tuxedo for his wedding. The tuxedo cost $125.

Mario testified that the wedding went well and he and his bride left for the balance of their holiday.

Throughout the two months he kept in touch with Conair by email but received no reports about his lost luggage.

During his trip, he said he was obliged to buy toiletries and more clothes at a cost of $368. He produced receipts for all these items.

When he returned to Toronto, there was a notice in his apartment mailbox from Conair. It said his luggage was in the storage area at the airport and could be picked up or delivered by Conair. He told the company to deliver it.

Sarah Fitzgerald, representing Conair, testified that the company did everything possible to assist Mario and she apologized for the dilemma in which he found himself.

She said if the luggage had been lost permanently Mario would only be entitled to the amount specified on his ticket under the Warsaw Convention, which governs losses of luggage by air passengers. She added that the luggage had not been lost but only misplaced.

Conair was prepared to pay Mario $400 for the inconvenience, but she said Mario refused the offer.

On cross-examination by Mario as to where the luggage was for two months, she said she received a report from the company that handles the baggage for Conair in Toronto and that the luggage had been directed to customs for examination and then put in storage. Apparently, according to Fitzgerald, the customs people were suspicious of the large number of suitcases. She added that their suspicion was further enhanced because Mario had an extensive criminal record. This bit of information is irrelevant and will be ignored by me.

The question to be decided: whether Conair is responsible for Mario's expenses and, if so, how much?

You be the judge.

JANE ROSS

VS.

GORDON GREGORY

OPENING STATEMENT

The plaintiff, Jane Ross, is suing for damage to the walls and floors of the recreation room in a house she bought from the defendant, Gordon Gregory.

THE EVIDENCE

In May 2008, Jane Ross bought a bungalow on Pleasant Road in Meaford, Ontario. The house number is 1938. This was, according to the plaintiff, a beautiful three-bedroom bungalow on one of the nicer streets in town. The basement was finished with wood panelling and carpeted. The purchase price of the house was $328,000. The plaintiff said the price was very high compared to others in the area but she had fallen in love with the house, especially the finished basement, which is the subject of the claim.

The plaintiff testified that she didn't move into the house on closing as she hadn't yet sold the house she had been living in for some years. Her agent told her it would be easier to sell if the furniture was there and the house looked lived in.

On cross-examination she admitted that the new house on Pleasant Road remained vacant for about three months from late May until early September.

She also admitted that she turned the hydro off at the main panel in an effort to save electricity.

She knew the house was built very well and had an air exchanger system to remove humidity from the house. This was one of the reasons she felt the basement recreation room would not be damp.

About every two weeks she would visit the new house to make sure everything was okay. After about a week, she noticed a smell in the basement but attributed it to the house being closed up.

She admitted also under cross-examination that she didn't bother looking into the basement on her visits to her house as the hydro was off and she was nervous about going down into the dark basement.

In early September, having sold her house, she moved into 1938 Pleasant Road and went to the electric panel in the basement to turn on the hydro. She was very upset to find the carpeting wet and the wood panelling damp to the touch.

She called in a company that did restoration work in flooded and fire-damaged houses and they told her that the carpet was beyond fixing and that some of the wall panels were warping and should be replaced.

Jane had the carpet replaced and because she was unable to find a matching wood panelling she had to have the walls refinished. The total cost of these repairs was $8,250.

On completion of the repairs, Jane had her lawyer write a letter to Gordon Gregory demanding compensation.

Her statement of claim and the lawyer's letter set out the fact that the defendant signed a statement with the real estate agent indicating there had never been water in the basement.

The defence to her claim was based on one point and that is that on taking possession the plaintiff turned off the hydro shutting down the air exchanger.

Gregory called a witness, Silas Short, whom I determined on examination to be an expert witness able to give evidence on home contractors.

Short said that on examining the house he determined that it was airtight. He said many new homes, especially those built within the last 10 years, would have moisture problems for a few years until the building materials dried sufficiently for the moisture problems to end.

Gregory said in his testimony that he never had any moisture problems, but added that the air exchanger system had run continuously from the time he bought the house and moved in.

Clarifying this point, Short said that he believed the problem arose because the plaintiff shut off the hydro.

The question to be determined: whether the plaintiff is entitled to recover her expenses for the repair of the basement recreation room?

You be the judge.

CARMAN BISERI

VS.

JACK GEORGE

OPENING STATEMENT

The plaintiff, Carman Biseri, is suing the defendant, Jack George, for reimbursement of monies paid under a lease.

THE EVIDENCE

George is the owner of a commercial property, more particularly a store on the main street of Orangeville, Ontario.

He occupied the property, running a tile and carpet store, before retiring in 1995. Subsequently, he rented it out for various purposes.

Usually, George had his lawyer draw up a lease for whatever period the parties agreed upon.

In 2003 the store was leased to Biseri for two years at a monthly rent of $1,800. One of the clauses in the lease was that Biseri would be responsible for insuring for liability and for fire on the contents.

Biseri would also be responsible for reimbursing the defendant for fire insurance on the building. During the two-year period of the rental, this amounted to $3,600 per year as the defendant billed Biseri $300 each month, which was added onto the rent of $1,800 per month for a total of $2,100.

All went well during the two years.

At the end of the two years, Biseri sold the business to a friend, Eric Carmeli, and a new lease was negotiated with George.

The new lease between Carmeli and George provided that the rent would be $2,000 per month and that George would pay for the fire coverage on his building. George testified he made this change because his insurance agent found a cheaper insurance.

Approximately three months into the new lease Biseri found out from his friend, Carmeli, that Carmeli was getting a better deal than he had.

Biseri approached George and told him he wanted a rebate of $100 per month. George refused to talk about it.

Biseri then wrote to George and demanded a refund or he would start court proceedings. George ignored the letter and that is why we are dealing with this matter today.

The question to be decided: whether the plaintiff is entitled to a refund of $100 per month for the higher insurance charge he paid while he was a tenant?

You be the judge.

JANICE GOOD

VS.

QUICK LOAN INC.

OPENING STATEMENT

Janice Good is suing Quick Loan Inc. for excessive charges made to her as a result of a loan.

THE EVIDENCE

Good is a single mother with two children, ages nine and seven, who works at Erin Prefab Houses Inc., where she gets paid biweekly.

Janice testified that she frequently finds herself in financial difficulty. She receives no support from her former husband who spends a lot of time in jail.

On September 7, about eight days before she would receive her cheque from Erin Prefab, she indicated she needed some money to enrol her seven-year-old son in hockey. Apparently there was a deadline for his enrolment.

Janice went to the storefront operation of Quick Loan and enquired about an advance on her paycheque. Some of her friends had used the service so Janice knew something about it.

Quick Loan was quick to lend her money based on her expected paycheque in about eight days. She signed a form that gave Quick Loan the right to cash her cheque, which she indicated would be $700, after deductions, for the two-week period.

She also signed some other forms, which, she said, she didn't read. Quick Loan gave her $525 cash. This meant that it was charging her $175 for an eight-day loan.

When Janice's paycheque came, it had been reduced by $60 for a uniform, which the company required her to have. She said that this was a twice-a-year deduction and she had forgotten about it.

Quick Loan was very nasty with her and said it would loan her the additional money, but she would have to pay a service charge of $75. So the loan of $60 quickly became $130 plus interest totalling $155.

Janice, once again, signed the necessary forms provided to her by Quick Loan.

When Erin Prefab was notified about the assignment of Janice's pay to Quick Loan, she was called in by the human resources department for an interview. They apparently had had previous dealings with Quick Loan and advised Janice of the exorbitant rate of interest and suggested she sue Quick Loan for usury — an excessively high rate of interest.

Janice took her employer's advice and began the action and Quick Loan filed a defence.

Quick Loan explained that its service charges were the same for everyone because of the paperwork involved. The company also testified that it had to charge the high interest because many clients defaulted in their loans and it had to get paid by someone.

When I questioned Quick Loan about its interest rate, the response was that it was standard. The company also testified that Janice still owed it money and it was counterclaiming for that.

The questions to be decided: whether Janice should be refunded the interest and service charges she made even if she signed, agreeing to them, and whether Quick Loan should receive the money it claims?

You be the judge.

26

DOROTHY MCKAY

VS.

JAMES HARRINGTON, CARRYING ON BUSINESS AS WELLINGTON STABLES

OPENING STATEMENT

The plaintiff, Dorothy McKay, is suing to recover money paid to the defendant, James Harrington, for a horse that the plaintiff says was unsound.

THE EVIDENCE

The plaintiff and her daughter were very interested in horses and, in particular, barrel racing with horses.

After seeing an ad in the *Guelph Ontario Tribune*, the plaintiff went to Wellington Stables and viewed a horse known as Jocko. Jocko was a quarter horse and appeared to be in good condition (horse people say such a horse is "sound").

The plaintiff and defendant came to an agreed price of $6,800, which the plaintiff would pay after getting a medical approval from her veterinarian, Dr. Jack Hughes. Hughes had provided veterinary services to McKay over a number of years and said he would go to Wellington Stables and examine Jocko. This was agreeable to Harrington.

In the meantime, Harrington got in touch with his veterinarian who examined Jocko and gave a letter indicating from his examination that Jocko seemed sound.

Hughes examined Jocko on behalf of the plaintiff, and was satisfied that the horse was in good condition.

Before accepting the plaintiff's cheque, Harrington advised her that Jocko had one more show for which he had paid the entry fee and that was at the Royal Agricultural Winter Fair in Toronto.

That event was about two weeks away. McKay said that arrangement was fine as she had to make some changes to her barn before Jocko could move in.

The whole McKay family, including Dorothy's mother, Jane, who was also interested in horses, having been raised on a farm, decided to go to the Royal and watch the barrel racing competition. James Harrington was to ride Jocko.

The first indication of a problem with Jocko occurred when he was rounding the first barrel on the course. Jocko seemed to have a problem with making the turn. Part way through the second race Jane, who was a bit of a barrel racer in her own day, noticed Jocko again had some trouble rounding several of the barrels.

After the race Dorothy and her mother went to the barn where Jocko was located and talked to Harrington. Dorothy mentioned that Jocko seemed to be having trouble on the turns.

Harrington said it wasn't Jocko's fault but his. He said that he had had a serious hernia operation about 10 days before and was unable to use his legs to control Jocko.

Dorothy testified that she was satisfied with that explanation and agreed to pick up Jocko on the following weekend.

Once the horse was at the McKay farm, Dorothy and her daughter, Lillie, took turns every day exercising Jocko in a paddock next to the barn.

Once again they noticed that Jocko was having a problem.

Dorothy testified that it seemed like Jocko's rear end didn't know what the front end was doing and was becoming less agile with every outing.

The plaintiff phoned the defendant about this but he denied having any problems with Jocko.

McKay advised the court that there was an unwritten guarantee among horse dealers that if a horse appeared not to be sound then it would be taken back. She called a witness, Joyce Lattimer, a dealer in horses who confirmed the guarantee.

Harrington, however, said that both veterinarians had looked at Jocko and certified him sound and he refused McKay's request to return Jocko and give a refund.

The plaintiff then decided to go one step further and made arrangements to have the horse examined at the Veterinary College in Guelph.

Jocko was left at the clinic at the college for the vets to examine and two days later McKay received a call to come and pick him up.

At the college, Dr. James Sniderman and Dr. Henry Forshaw handed McKay a report on their findings and told her that Jocko was indeed a sick horse. Their report indicated that Jocko had what is commonly known as Wobbler's disease. Dr. Sniderman was called as a witness for McKay and, after hearing his credentials, I accepted him as an expert witness. Dr. Sniderman was a licensed veterinarian with two post-graduate degrees in neurology from the University of Guelph and Michigan State Veterinary College.

He said there was no cure for Wobbler's disease and the horse would ultimately be so crippled that it wouldn't be able to get up or lie down.

In his testimony, Harrington denied any knowledge of Jocko's problems. He also relied on the certificates of the two vets that said Jocko appeared to be sound.

When I questioned Dr. Sniderman about the vets' reports, he said that there was no way an ordinary practicing vet would be able to make the diagnosis.

The question to be decided: whether McKay should be able to return the horse and get her money back?

You be the judge.

27

Stan John

vs.

Jack Star Cleaners

Opening Statement

The plaintiff, Stan John, is suing the defendant, Jack Star Cleaners, for $750 for damages to a special Native-made sports jacket.

The Evidence

On September 4, 2008, while visiting friends in Shelburne, Ontario, Stan took his hand-made jacket to Jack Star Cleaners for dry cleaning. John gave testimony that his jacket had some grease stains. Apparently, on his way from Sioux Lookout to Shelburne, his car's fan belt broke, and, in the process of installing a new one, John got some grease on the jacket's sleeves.

John produced his jacket which appeared to be made of bear skin and was beautifully embroidered. He said it was made by persons of Native origin running a small co-operative in Sioux Lookout and that he paid $750 for the jacket.

I observed that the jacket was dyed a creamy-white colour and that the embroidery, which was on the front and back and down the sleeves, was coming off the jacket in several places.

The plaintiff said that Jack Star, who advertised cleaning in 24 hours, had examined the somewhat unusual jacket and, when questioned by John, had said that there would be no problem. His exact words were that Star said, "we do this type of coat frequently." John said that the jacket was only three weeks old and he produced a receipt to show the purchase price which was, in fact, $750. There was no tax, as John's purchases were tax exempt because of his Native status.

Apart from the loose embroidery, the plaintiff said that Jack Star Cleaners had shrunk the jacket so he was no longer able to get it on. I asked him to demonstrate his inability to get it on and it was obvious that it was too small for him.

On cross-examination by Star's lawyer, John said it was, in fact, his jacket and that he did, in fact, wear it all the way from Sioux Lookout to Shelburne. He got the grease on it just outside Huntsville.

The defence for the defendant was to the effect that it never guaranteed that a fabric wouldn't shrink. Star testified that he had dry cleaned several similar jackets and never had any problems. He said that when John picked up the jacket and complained about the condition, he asked for the jacket back to have it tested by a lab that does work for dry cleaners. Star said that the report from the lab was that there was no shrinkage and that the embroidery was inadequately done.

When I asked him for a copy of the report, he was unable to produce it.

The question to be decided: whether Jack Star Cleaners is responsible for the damage, if any, to the jacket or whether Stan John took his chances in having an unusual item of clothing dry cleaned?

You be the judge.

28

Timothy Sheerwood

vs.

John Grant, Carrying on Business as Grant's Parking

Opening Statement

The plaintiff, Timothy Sheerwood, is suing the defendant, John Grant, for $10,000 for the loss of his car parked at Grant's parking lot, including the cost of a rental vehicle.

The Evidence

Grant's Parking runs a parking lot on Lakeshore Road in Port Credit. The lot is near a GO Train station and many commuters to Toronto park in Grant's lot. There is a sign on the side of the shed that John Grant uses as an office, indicating what the hourly and daily rates are for parking.

Sheerwood left his car with the keys in it for Grant to park for the day on October 14, 2008. The vehicle was a 1998 Plymouth van. It was left at about 7:30 a.m.

The plaintiff testified that he had been in the habit of leaving his car at the lot almost daily for about one year. The lot was able to accommodate about 80 cars.

When Sheerwood returned around 5:30 p.m., he went to the office to get his keys and was advised by John Grant that the keys were in the car and that the car was in the back row near the back of the lot.

The plaintiff went in the direction pointed out by Grant, but couldn't find his vehicle. He returned to the office and Grant went with him to find the van.

It didn't take more than five minutes for both parties to realize that the van was gone. Grant returned to the office with Sheerwood close behind and Grant phoned the police to report the van stolen.

In about 15 minutes two police cars appeared on the lot and the officers took down the details from both the plaintiff and defendant. Sheerwood went home in a taxi.

For the next three weeks Sheerwood rented a car and began a search for a replacement vehicle. He finally settled on another similar Plymouth van for which he paid $9,250.

When the plaintiff approached Grant for reimbursement, Grant refused, saying that the vehicle was left at the owner's risk. A letter from Sheerwood's lawyer demanding payment was ignored and at that point Sheerwood began this action.

The question to be decided: whether Grant is responsible for the loss of the vehicle and, if so, can Sheerwood succeed in obtaining judgment for $10,000 he claims?

You be the judge.

29

PROGRESS HARDWOOD FLOORING INC.

VS.

CHARLES AND EVA SPANNING

OPENING STATEMENT

The plaintiff, Progress Hardwood Flooring Inc., is suing the defendants, Charles and Eva Spanning, for an account for unpaid hardwood flooring installed by Progress. The defendants are countersuing for the cost of replacing the work done by Progress.

THE EVIDENCE

Progress and the Spannings entered into a contract for the supply and installation of cherry hardwood flooring in the Spanning residence at 7 Ironwood Avenue in Mississauga. The residence is a large custom-built home of approximately 3,500 square feet in an upscale area of Mississauga.

The Spannings had the house built 14 years ago and at that time had carpet installed in the living room, dining room, and den. Eva Spanning testified that the carpet was worn and they decided to replace it with hardwood. After shopping around they decided to have Progress do the work and entered into a contract. The cost of the work, including all materials and the ripping up and disposal of the carpeting, was to be

$9,350. A deposit of $1,000 was paid and Progress ordered the hardwood and in about three weeks came to do the job.

Charles Spanning said that the installation was completed in about 10 days around the end of August. He said that the workers were neat and tidy and left the home in spotless condition. The Spannings left for their Muskoka cottage the day before the work was completed. When they returned two weeks later, they found the bill from Progress but noticed the cherry flooring was warping in a number of places. Charles phoned Progress and advised the company of the problem and Progress told him it would be over to look at the floor in a few days. The Spannings decided then to withhold payment of the balance owing.

Around the end of September, James Wiffle of Progress came to the house and examined the flooring. He testified that he had been in this line of business for over 26 years and that he couldn't see that there was any problem that wouldn't rectify itself. He said the cherry wood probably had a higher moisture content than most hardwood and until the heat was turned on in the house the problem would probably remain. When cross-examined by the lawyer for the Spannings, Wiffle admitted that the house had an air exchanger, which usually would take out the humidity in a few days.

At this point the Spannings said that the heat had been on since they returned from their cottage in mid-September and the heat exchanger was on all the time. They said they never had moisture problems in their house and their windows never had moisture on them.

The Spannings decided to wait for three or four weeks to see if the hardwood dried and settled down and advised Progress that they intended to withhold the balance owing until they were satisfied.

Following that conversation with Progress, Wiffle said he would wait for three weeks and, if the Spannings' bill was still unpaid, he would seek legal advice.

Charles Spanning testified that by mid-December the heat had been on in the house for three months, the air exchanger had been on, and the flooring was still warped. Phone calls to Progress went unanswered.

In mid-January Progress began court action for recovery of the $8,350 it was owed.

On receipt of the plaintiff's claim on January 20, the Spannings consulted their lawyer and were advised to obtain an estimate for the repair and replacement of the flooring and to do so promptly, so that they could file a defence and counterclaim within the required 20 days.

Called as a witness for the Spannings was Tom Lawson, a contractor, who testified he had been installing hardwood floors for 35 years. He said he couldn't believe the condition of the flooring, which he indicated was extremely expensive. He said he tested the moisture content on January 31 with his hydrometer and found it to be extremely high. When asked about this by me, he said it was his opinion that the cherry hardwood had not been properly dried.

Lawson recommended that Spannings have the floors redone at a cost of $11,500 including ripping up the existing hardwood installed by Progress. The Spannings chose to take his advice.

Their counterclaim is for $3,150, being $1,000 for their deposit plus $2,150 being the extra cost of Lawson's work over and above that of Progress.

The issues to be decided: First, is Progress entitled to the balance of its contract price, namely $8,350? Second, are the defendants entitled to have their deposit returned and to receive $2,150 for the extra cost of having Tom Lawson redo the work?

You be the judge.

30

John and Sarah Shapiro

vs.

Airport Management Inc.

Opening Statement

The plaintiffs, John and Sarah Shapiro, are suing the defendant, Airport Management Inc., for damages to a laptop computer damaged at the airport's inspection and security facility.

The Evidence

The computer in question belongs to John Shapiro who lent it to his daughter, Sarah, who is a student at the University of British Columbia. Sarah has custody of the computer while she is attending school. Her home is in Caledon, Ontario, and she had been home for the Christmas holidays. She brought the computer home from university as she was working on assignments during the holidays.

On January 8, 2008, she went to the airport to catch her flight back to Vancouver. As usual, she had the computer in a carrying case inside her main carry-on bag.

At the security checkpoint she was advised to take the computer out of her bag and put it though the X-ray screening and she complied with that request.

Sarah testified that there had been a long line-up for security checks and many people were asked to remove their shoes and empty their pockets and put these items in the bucket supplied by Airport Management.

Sarah said she put her computer on the track along with her purse and shoes in a bucket.

The security staff was extremely busy and things seemed to back up with the inspector, and particularly with the X-raying of computers and other items.

Sarah testified that once her computer had gone through the X-ray machine, the staff person on the receiving end of the track seemed overwhelmed with all the shoes and buckets that were piling up.

At that point the staff person gave a number of items on the track a big push to get them out of the way and in the process knocked her computer off the table and it crashed on the floor. As she was in a hurry to catch her flight, Sarah did not examine the computer until she was on the plane. At that point she found that the screen was cracked and there appeared to be damage to the keyboard.

On arriving in Vancouver she took the computer to a computer fix-it store and was advised that it was a write-off. She phoned her father, John, and he told her to keep the broken computer, but to purchase on his credit card a similar model for her use at school.

John testified that Sarah bought a similar model for $1,218. The exact model of the broken computer was no longer available as it was two years old.

The representative from Airport Management, Carlos Singh, said that it would be impossible for any employee to knock a computer off the table. He did not have the employee in question in court to testify.

On questioning by John Shapiro, he admitted he was not present and didn't really know what happened, but asserted that all persons going through the checkpoint were responsible for the safety of their belongings. He also stated that the price paid for the new computer was excessive.

John had previously testified that the new computer cost about $300 less than the old broken one.

Singh said that there is a sign on the wall at the entrance to the security checkpoint indicating that passengers are responsible for their belongings. Sarah said that she did not see the sign.

The question to be decided: whether the defendant is responsible for the damage and, if so, the quantum of damages, or whether, in view of the alleged sign, Airport Management is absolved of liability?

You be the judge.

31

APARTMENT RENTALS INC.

VS.

DIANE SAWYER

OPENING STATEMENT

The plaintiff, Apartment Rentals Inc., is suing the defendant, Diane Sawyer, for arrears of rent and for damage to an apartment.

THE EVIDENCE

On July 1, 2006, the plaintiff rented an apartment to the defendant at 70 Mill Street in Orangeville. The rent was $640 per month, plus utilities. The defendant moved in and paid the first month's rent and promised to pay the last month's rent when she received her mother's allowance.

Diane Sawyer is a single mother with an eight-month-old child. She testified that the father of the child refused to pay for support and she was living on welfare.

She admitted she didn't pay for the last month's rent and the rent for the next seven months. She did put the hydro account in her name when she moved in, but, after falling in arrears with the monthly hydro bill, the hydro commission threatened to cut off the hydro. Apparently they did on several occasions until she came up with the money.

In January, 2007, the plaintiff landlord applied to the Rental Housing Tribunal to have Sawyer evicted from the apartment.

The landlord obtained an order to have her evicted, but then had to file the order with the court and apply to the sheriff to enforce the Order of Eviction.

The plaintiff said that this process cost over $700 and, by the time the tenant was locked out of the apartment, she owed nine months' rent.

The plaintiff testified that when he regained possession of the apartment all the defendant's possessions were still in it and he had to have them removed. He also said the apartment was a mess and had to be repainted.

In the process of repainting the apartment the landlord noticed a hole about two inches in diameter drilled through the floor into the basement laundry room.

The plaintiff suspected that the defendant had drilled the hole and run an electrical cord into the laundry room and tapped into an electric outlet in the laundry room.

On checking with the hydro office the plaintiff was advised that the hydro had been cut off for non-payment of Diane's bill in December and was never turned on again.

The defendant testified that she knew she was in arrears in her rent, but denied any knowledge of the application to have her evicted. She also vehemently denied tapping into the laundry-room electricity.

On cross-examination by the solicitor for the plaintiff she denied all knowledge of the hole through the floor, but she couldn't explain how she was able to keep her refrigerator and lights on when the hydro had been cut off.

The landlord had a separate bill for the laundry room and the outside lights and he determined that for several months the bill had doubled over the usual amounts he paid.

The question to be determined: whether Diane is responsible for the hydro, the removal of possessions, the clean up of the apartment, and the past due rent?

You be the judge.

Arnold Whitney

vs.

Valley View Farms Inc.

Opening Statement

The plaintiff, Arnold Whitney, is suing Valley View Farms Inc., the defendant, for $7,321 for damage to his BMW.

The Evidence

Whitney was driving along County Road 140 near the Village of Drayton, Ontario, on March 4, 2009. The weather was clear — there was no rain — and it was about 6:30 in the evening. The sun had set and it was almost dark. The road was a two-lane gravel road.

Whitney testified that he was about half a mile from the village and travelling at about 60 miles or 100 kilometres per hour.

The plaintiff said that he travelled this stretch of road daily on his way home from work in Brampton when, suddenly and without warning, a Holstein cow ran out of the ditch in front of his vehicle. The cow was killed and considerable damage was done to the plaintiff's car.

The defendant's farm company was represented by Darly Sneider who, along with his brother, Darren, owned the farm from which the cow had wandered. Valley View ran a large dairy operation with some 350 cows and owned three farms all fronting on County Road 140.

Sneider did not deny that the cow was part of Valley View's herd. He testified that with 350 cows it was not unusual for one to periodically break through a fence and get onto the road. He said that every couple of days he checked to see if the fences were intact and that particular section of fence had been checked the morning of the accident. He said he was sorry for the damage to the plaintiff's car, but, that if Whitney had been driving at a more reasonable speed, he could have avoided hitting the cow.

Whitney produced a paid invoice for $7,321 for the repair work on his BMW.

The defendant also testified that there was a hill, which would block the plaintiff's view, approximately 200 feet from the scene of the impact.

Whitney on cross-examination by Sneider vehemently denied he was driving faster than 100 kilometres per hour and said there was no hill but agreed there was a moderate incline over which he would have been driving before he struck the cow.

The question to be answered: whether the defendant farm company is responsible for the accident because of the disrepair of the fence or whether the plaintiff is responsible as a result of not using due care and attention while driving along the rural road?

It is interesting to note that the defendant did not make a claim for the loss of the cow.

You be the judge.

John Grey

vs.

Fred Grey

Opening Statement

John Grey is suing Fred Grey for half of the cost of a fence erected between their farms. He is also claiming for loss of his corn crop. Fred is counterclaiming for half the cost of an electric fence he installed.

The Evidence

John Grey has a 100-acre farm, being lot seven, concession five in Caledon, and his brother, Fred Grey, has the farm immediately to the south of John, being lot six, concession seven, Caledon.

Both farms are what is commonly known as "string 100s." That is to say, both farms run all the way from one concession road to the next.

This is somewhat unusual as normally in Caledon most farms would have a frontage of about 1,980 feet and a depth of 2,200 feet, making 100 acres.

In this case the brothers both have long, narrow farms each with a frontage of 990 feet and depth of 4,400 feet.

The brothers appear to have gotten along with each

other, with each basically cash cropping, that is to say, growing oats, wheat, hay, barley, and corn, which they harvest and sell. The evidence was that they had to some extent shared equipment in their operations.

In the spring of 2007 Fred Grey decided he was going to convert his barn and operation into a dairy business and was able to obtain a quota from the Ontario Milk Marketing Board, which would enable him to have approximately 100 cows.

Trouble between the two brothers started shortly after Fred got his cows and the cows wandered over onto John's property, trampling his corn and wheat. John spoke to Fred and Fred agreed to erect an electric fence down the line between their farms, but only for about 1,000 feet. He said his cows never went to the back of the farm and that he was not prepared to extend the fence further.

John testified that Fred's cows did, in fact, go back further and went around the end of the electric fence and destroyed about 12 acres of his corn crop.

John again approached his brother to see if the problem could be resolved and Fred told John that he would not extend the fence any further. At this point the brothers stopped speaking to each other.

John said his loss during the 2007 crop year was more than $1,080 based on total loss of corn, which should have yielded 120 bushels per acre.

In the fall of 2007, John began construction of a five-strand wire fence between the farms, starting at the end of Fred's electric fence and running to the back of the farm. This was a distance of 3,400 feet.

When the fence was completed, he presented Fred with a bill of $3,780, being half the cost of the fence. John said Fred ripped up the bill, threw it at him and told him to get off his property.

John testified he was totally frustrated by his brother's reaction and realized that their previous friendly relationship was at an end.

He consulted a lawyer and proceeded to bring this action.

In his defence Fred said he didn't believe his cows were causing any damage and he felt the erection of the electric fence was all he should do to control his cows. He said he wanted $1,250 from John for half the cost of the electric fence he installed.

The questions to be decided: first, what, if anything, should John receive for his crop loss, second, what can he obtain from Fred for the erection of the fence, and third, can Fred be reimbursed for half the cost of his electric fence?

You be the judge.

34

SANDRA AND GEORGE SILTON

VS.

MARIA JACOBSON

OPENING STATEMENT

The plaintiffs, Sandra and George Silton, are suing the defendant, Maria Jacobson, for $4,600, the cost of items they allege were to be left in the house they purchased from the defendant.

THE EVIDENCE

The parties entered into an agreement of purchase and sale for the property known as 24 Agnes Street in the City of Mississauga.

The transaction was to close on June 1, 2006, and, in fact, did close on that date.

The agreement contained a clause allowing the purchasers, the Siltons, to inspect the property the day before closing, which they, in fact, did.

A clause in the agreement indicated that the offer included the stove and refrigerator and the washer and dryer. The plaintiffs testified that when they did their inspection all the items that were there when they signed the offer were still there the day of the inspection.

On June 1 the deal was closed by the respective lawyers and the Siltons picked up the key at their lawyer's office at about 3:30 in the afternoon.

On arrival at their new home the Siltons were surprised to find that the appliances they thought they were getting had been substituted with others. Sandra Stilton said that all the appliances were older and of different makes than those they were supposed to receive. Sandra said the Maytag washer and dryer were replaced with General Electric models, the stove, which was to be a Moffat, was replaced with an Admiral, and the Maytag refrigerator was replaced with a Danby.

Sandra testified that she was 71.

On cross-examination by Jacobson's lawyer, he tried to suggest that because of her age, she probably forgot what she had seen on the inspection. She replied that she knew appliances and was far from being senile.

Sandra said the appliances left in the house weren't the ones that were to be included.

Maria Jacobson testified that she did replace the refrigerator because the Maytag was not working well and she felt she should replace it.

Sandra said all the replacements looked to her like they were picked up at a used appliance store.

She testified that she phoned the lawyer who acted for them and he said he would contact the defendant's lawyer immediately to find out what was going on. He got back to Sandra about two hours later and said that he got the word from Jacobson's lawyer that his client denied any switching of the appliances.

As a result of the defendant's position the plaintiffs went out and purchased four new appliances at a cost of $4,600. They also had their lawyer write to the defendant's lawyer advising that the four appliances she left would be put in the garage and could be picked up by her within the next three weeks, after which they would be put in the garbage.

The answer to this case to a large extent centres around the credibility of the witnesses because of the conflicting evidence.

You be the judge.

35

JACK'S GARAGE INC.

VS.

RALPH MENZIE

OPENING STATEMENT

The plaintiff, Jack's Garage Inc., is suing the defendant, Ralph Menzie, for the cost of installing a new transmission in his 1989 Dodge. The cost of the job was $2,383. Menzie is counterclaiming for $2,830 for having to have his vehicle fixed at another garage.

THE EVIDENCE

Ralph Menzie took his 1989 Dodge to a local garage in Stratford, Ontario. He said he had dealt with Jack's Garage on several previous occasions and was satisfied with what Jack had done.

In July of 2008, Menzie discovered that he was having transmission problems and he took his car to Jack's for advice and an estimate. Jack confirmed Menzie's belief about the transmission and gave him an estimate of $1,800 to replace the transmission including all labour and taxes.

Menzie said he went to another garage for another estimate, but decided to have Jack do the work.

On July 20 he left his car at Jack's.

Jack explained he had to order the transmission from a parts supplier and it didn't arrive until about July 26.

As soon as the transmission arrived, Jack began work on the car and completed it within three days. During the course of working on the transmission, he found several related problems and phoned Menzie about them and he said Menzie agreed to the extra cost.

He testified that the extras, amounting to $583, were the reason his bill was $2,383 instead of the original estimate of $1,800.

Jack also testified that Menzie had signed a work order for the original cost of $1,800, but he took Menzie's verbal agreement that Menzie would pay the additional amount.

When the work was completed, Menzie gave Jack's Garage a cheque for $2,383.

On the same day he picked up the car, Menzie drove up to Milverton about 26 miles from his home near Stratford. He parked his car on his son's driveway and, when he came out to go home about three hours after arriving, he noticed a big puddle of oil on the driveway. On looking under his car he determined that the oil was coming from his transmission. He immediately went to his bank in Stratford and stopped payment on his cheque to the garage.

When Menzie phoned Jack to advise him of the oil leak, he also told him he had stopped payment on the cheque.

Jack refused to have anything more to do with Menzie and within the next few days commenced this action.

Menzie, meanwhile, took his car to another garage that specialized in transmissions. Larry Schmidt of Fast Transmissions testified on behalf of Menzie that the work done by Jack was inferior and said that the transmission installed by Jack was the wrong one.

The question to be decided: should Jack be entitled to his claim for $2,383 and should Menzie be successful in his counterclaim for $2,830 for having his transmission fixed at another garage?

You be the judge.

36

Robert Howard

vs.

We Park — You Fly

Opening Statement

The plaintiff, Robert Howard, is suing the defendant, We Park — You Fly, for $2,715 for damage to his car while it was in the care of the defendant at the Hamilton, Ontario, airport.

The Evidence

Howard, who is a resident of Burlington, Ontario, drove to the Hamilton airport for a flight to Winnipeg. The defendant operates a large parking facility for air travellers. Howard left his 2006 Lexus with the keys in it at the front office for a valet parking service. He entered the check-in office, signed the appropriate forms, left an imprint of his credit card, and advised the clerk that he would be returning the next day.

When Howard returned the next day, the car jockey brought the car to the front door. Howard had already paid for the parking. When he came outside with his luggage, he noticed that the front of the car had been hit or had hit something, causing extensive damage that he testified had not been there when he left the car for parking by the defendant's company.

When Howard went back into the front office, he said he

was advised that the vehicle had the dent when he left it and that, even if there wasn't a dent at that time, the defendant took no responsibility, as it clearly stated on the ticket that they took no responsibility for damage or theft to any vehicle.

Having received no satisfaction from the clerk, Howard wrote a letter to the manager of the defendant's company advising him of his concern and demanding that the defendant repair the damage.

At the end of three weeks, no reply was received by the plaintiff from the defendant and the plaintiff commenced this action for the estimated cost of the repair, which was $2,715.

At trial the defendant repeated its position of non-liability based on the parking ticket. The defendant's witness, Jeffrey White, said that he parked the car at the edge of the defendant's property. On cross-examination by Howard's solicitor he admitted that when he left the car it seemed to roll forward a bit toward a chain-link fence. He said that the brakes in the Lexus seemed to be defective.

Howard produced a mechanic, Jack Smart, from his Lexus dealer who said that he checked the vehicle at the required maintenance times and when last at the garage, eight days before Howard's trip, everything was in working order. He also said that Howard brought his vehicle to the dealership after the defence was filed alleging defective brakes, and that the rotors and pads were in excellent condition. The car only had 17,000 kilometres on it at the time of the inspection.

When I asked him if the engine was turned off, could the car slide down the slope, he said it was virtually impossible.

The questions to be answered: first, did the car jockey, Jeffrey White, drive the Lexus into the fence thereby causing the damage to the grill as claimed by Howard, and, second, if he did, was the waiver of liability on the parking ticket sufficient to absolve the defendant of liability?

You be the judge.

37

Gordon Snelgrove

vs.

Union Insurance Co.

Opening Statement

The plaintiff, Gordon Snelgrove, is suing the defendant, Union Insurance Co., for payment under his insurance policy as a result of a claim arising from an accident.

The Evidence

Snelgrove was the owner of a 1997 GMC dump truck valued at $8,550 that was totally destroyed when hit by a train on the outskirts of Milton on March 10, 2003. Snelgrove was seriously injured in the accident. While Snelgrove was recovering in hospital in Toronto, the defendant had an appraisal firm investigate the accident and in the course of this investigation interviewed the plaintiff.

As a result of the information dug up by the appraiser, the defendant insurer denied liability under its policy and in a letter to the plaintiff enclosed a cheque for $1,774, being the total premium that the plaintiff had paid for insurance.

The defendant's witness, Klaus Statboom, testified that he determined that Snelgrove, in whose name the policy was held, had transferred the truck to a limited company called

Gordon Snelgrove Incorporated. This company is owned solely by Gordon Snelgrove.

The defendant contends that because the policy is in the name of Gordon Snelgrove and the truck is in the name of Gordon Snelgrove Incorporated that there is, in fact, no insurance coverage and the company has refused to pay.

The question: whether because the truck is owned by the incorporated company and the insurance is in the name of Gordon Snelgrove, can the defendant deny liability and refuse to pay?

You be the judge.

38

JAMES BEER

VS.

NORTHERN RAILWAY CO.

OPENING STATEMENT

The plaintiff, James Beer, is suing the defendant, Northern Railway Co., for $4,250 and costs for damage to his luggage.

THE EVIDENCE

The plaintiff purchased a ticket from the defendant for travel from Toronto to North Bay. At the time of purchasing his ticket, namely January 8, 2008, Beer checked his luggage, which included his clothing and a laptop computer, which he valued at $3,500. He did not take the train trip himself until the next day, January 9, 2008. His checked luggage was shipped on January 8.

The luggage reached North Bay on January 8 and was placed in a storage room in the station.

At about 8:00 a.m. on January 9 an explosion in the storage room totally destroyed all the stored items, including the luggage of the plaintiff.

The defendant gave evidence that the explosion was as a result of the defendant's boiler blowing up.

The defendant pointed out that the ticket indicated that liability is limited to $100 unless a greater value is declared by the ticket purchaser and an extra charge is paid. There was no dispute that no extra charge was paid, nor was any greater value declared.

The defendants contend that they were bailees and that they were not responsible for the explosion and therefore not liable for the plaintiff's loss. They said the boiler was inspected by qualified persons semi-annually and no problems had been found. The boiler was three years old.

The question to be decided: whether the defendant as a bailee is responsible for the damage the plaintiff suffered?

You be the judge.

39

LAWRENCE AITKEN

VS.

QUICK REPAIR AND TOWING INC.

OPENING STATEMENT

The plaintiff, Lawrence Aitken, is suing the defendant, Quick Repair and Towing, for what he alleges is a gross overcharge in its bill.

THE EVIDENCE

On December 12, 2008, at about 10:30 p.m., the plaintiff was driving his car west on Dundas Street, near Highway 10, when he was involved in a multiple car accident. The road was covered with ice and it was snowing heavily. Aitken's vehicle, a Toyota Camry, was the third car in a pile-up, which occurred when the driver of the car that was two ahead of him hit the centre median, spun around, and came to a stop. Considerable damage was done to the front and rear of Aitken's car and it was undriveable.

The police were called and appeared on the scene within a few minutes, as did half-a-dozen tow trucks. The evidence is that the tow-truck operators listen on their radios to the police radios and dash to the scene hoping for business.

On this occasion the police were not long sorting out the mess, and told all the drivers of incapacitated cars to get their vehicles off the road.

A driver from a Quick Repair and Towing truck introduced himself to Aitken. After a brief discussion, Aitken instructed him to tow the car to its garage.

After advising the tow-truck driver he would come to Quick Repair and Towing's lot the next day after contacting his insurance company, Aitken took a taxi home.

On the day after the accident Aitken did, in fact, contact his insurance company and they said they would look at the vehicle and decide what they wanted to do as far as repairs were concerned.

Three days later, the insurance company advised Arthur that it had received an estimate from the defendant, but considered it too high and wanted the car towed to another repair facility. The insurance company adjuster told Aitken to arrange to have his vehicle towed to that facility.

When Arthur phoned Quick Repair and Towing, they agreed to tow the vehicle but wanted to be paid for the towing from the scene of the accident and three days' storage. Their bill was $280 for towing the vehicle for three miles to their facility and $150 for each of the three days of storage.

Aitken said he told Quick Repair and Towing that the bill was ridiculous and that he wouldn't pay. The defendant said the vehicle wouldn't be released until they were paid. To stop storage charges, Arthur gave the defendant his credit card number. Another tow-truck company picked up the vehicle and took it to the insurance company's selected repair shop.

Arthur is suing for return of his money, namely $730, but agreed during his evidence to pay $300 reducing his claim to $430.

The plaintiff called as a witness, George Still, the owner of A and B Towing and Storage. Still said the charges by Quick Repair and Towing were excessive and he felt that his company would have charged $150 for towing and $20 per day for storage for a total of $210.

The defendant testified that their charges were fair and reasonable and were consistent with what the industry was charging.

The question to be decided: whether Aitken, having paid the $730, should have his money returned by the defendant?

You be the judge.

40

GORDON BOE

VS.

FIRE EQUIPMENT INC.

OPENING STATEMENT

The plaintiff, Gordon Boe, is suing the defendant, Fire Equipment Inc., for $35,000 for wrongful dismissal. The defence is that dismissal was justified. Boe agreed to reduce his claim to $10,000 to come within the jurisdiction of this court.

THE EVIDENCE

Gordon Boe was a 10-year employee of Fire Equipment Inc. His job basically was to travel around a large part of West Central Ontario servicing the company's fire equipment installed at offices, stores, and factories, et cetera. The job entailed checking fire alarms, fire extinguishers, and exit lights.

Boe testified that his territory was comparatively large and he was, therefore, unable to service his customers more than once a year. He said the company was aware of this and his weekly reports to head office showed precisely where he had been and what customers he had seen. The reports were used by head office to determine what amount was to be billed to customers.

He also said that the company paid him a salary of $60,000 each year, plus his fuel, restaurant, and hotel expenses while he was on the road.

He lived in Stratford, which was more or less central to his territory. If possible, he would return to Stratford rather than staying at company expense at some motel.

His territory went from Lake Huron on the west, to Lake Erie on the south, and north to Owen Sound. Hamilton was to the east, but he did not work in Hamilton city.

He further testified that he got along well with his boss in Toronto, who he didn't see for months at a time, and had received no complaints from the company.

After working for the company for about nine and three-quarter years, he was advised by the company in a letter sent to his Stratford home that his territory was being enlarged to include Hamilton and areas almost to the edge of Metropolitan Toronto and north to Barrie.

He said his first reaction was that it had to be a mistake and he phoned his boss, Ed Sharpe, and asked for clarification. Ed apparently had received instructions from the owner of Fire Equipment Inc.

Gordon said that he told Ed that it was impossible to service such a large area unless he did it every other year and to please communicate his displeasure to the owner and Ed said he would.

When Gordon returned to Stratford for the weekend, about four weeks later, there was a letter from head office advising him that he was considered uncooperative and his services were no longer required by the company. Enclosed with the letter was a cheque for $5,000 as severance pay.

Gordon brought this action to recover what he believed to be proper severance pay.

The company argued that Gordon's dismissal was for cause in refusing a company directive to expand his territory.

The question to be decided: whether Gordon's dismissal was for cause or was unjust and, in any case, what monetary amount should he have received from the company?

You be the judge.

41

JAMES CARSWELL

VS.

KING HOTEL INC.

OPENING STATEMENT

The plaintiff, James Carswell, is suing the defendant, King Hotel Inc., for $3,000 for injuries suffered while a guest of the hotel.

THE EVIDENCE

Carswell and his wife, Judy, were on a road trip from Halifax, Nova Scotia, to Niagara Falls, Ontario. They had been stopping frequently, enjoying the sights along the way. They had reached Oakville, Ontario, when they decided to stop. Carswell said they had a directory of hotels and picked the King Hotel as a place to spend the night. He said that the hotel was an older building but had a great deal of charm and had been recommended by some friends who had stayed there the previous year.

They checked into the hotel, which was not very busy, and were given what the hotel clerk described as a one-bedroom suite. It had been a hot, sticky day and James Carswell decided to have a shower before dinner. In the bathroom there was a shower stall as well as a shower in the bathtub. Carswell decided to use the shower stall for fear of falling in the bathtub.

He said there was no shower mat for the tub. The plaintiff said that he turned on the hot and cold taps to regulate the water flow and the temperature and then got into the shower. After a few minutes the water become cooler, and he turned up the hot tap to try and regulate the temperature. The water suddenly became very hot and, when Carswell attempted to turn the hot water down, the tap fell off. Carswell said he was being scalded by the hot water and got out of the shower stall. The steaming hot water continued to run and he tried to reach the tap by wrapping a towel over his arm and reaching for the tap on the floor of the shower. This attempt was a failure and the water was starting to overflow from the shower stall onto the tile floor of the bathroom as his washcloth blocked the drain. He called to his wife to phone the front desk for help and by the time she made the call the water was flowing onto the carpet in the living area. At this point Judy noticed that his arms and chest were red from the scalding and she rushed to put ice on the affected areas.

Carswell said a maintenance person came to their suite to investigate and left to go to the shut off in a cupboard down the hall. Several staff came in with shop vacs to suck up the water. Carswell added that Judy was becoming very agitated about her husband's burns and said she would take James to a hospital, which she had noticed near the hotel.

James said he saw a doctor almost immediately. The doctor examined his burns and applied salve and bandaged his arms and chest. He was told the burns on his chest were serious second-degree burns and that he should stay overnight so that he could be checked on. James said that the pain was getting worse and he agreed to stay.

The next morning a doctor looked at his burns and said he could be released, so he phoned Judy to come and pick him up. On leaving the hospital he was presented with a bill for $765. When he presented his Nova Scotia health card, he was told that it couldn't be accepted in Ontario and he then wrote a cheque.

Before checking out of the King Hotel, James spoke to the manager about his injuries and the hospital bill. The manager apologized for his injuries but said he could do nothing about the bill from the hospital.

Carswell then located the maintenance man who had commented on similar events and determined that his name was Oscar Schmidt.

Carswell then called Oscar Schmidt as a witness.

Schmidt said he was no longer an employee of the hotel and added he had been fired because of some loose taps after he had changed the washers on them. He added that he was not a certified plumber, but had been expected to do all the plumbing repairs in the hotel.

Carswell asked him if he remembered the flood caused by the hot water tap in his room. Schmidt said he certainly did. Carswell then asked him if he could confirm that the tap fell off, resulting in the burns to Carswell's chest and arms. Again Schmidt replied in the affirmative and added that that incident was one of the reasons he was let go.

The defendant was represented by the hotel manager, Jackson Smyth, who was sworn in to testify. He stated that he recalled the incident, but he felt the expenses of the plaintiff should have been covered by the coverage in his home province. He added that, even if they were not, that the plaintiff should have sued Schmidt as Schmidt was not an employee of King Hotel, but was a contract worker on a flat per diem allowance. The defendant did not have any other witnesses.

The questions to be resolved here: whether the plaintiff should recover his medical expenses, even though he may have provincial insurance that might cover them, and, second, whether he should have sued Oscar Schmidt instead of King Hotel Inc?

You be the judge.

42

GORDON SEEBORN

VS.

NORTHERN BLASTING INC.

OPENING STATEMENT

The plaintiff, Gordon Seeborn, is suing the defendant, Northern Blasting Inc., for $3,250 as a result of alleged damages to his home located at 12 Bushell Avenue.

THE EVIDENCE

Seeborn is the owner of 12 Bushell Avenue. He testified that his home was about 35 years old, and he had lived there since it was built. He said that his property backed onto an open space with no houses, but an active stone quarry was about 800 metres away. The quarry had been started about 10 years ago by the defendant and during that time had not been any kind of annoyance. Periodically there would be a blast and a slight rumble when the defendant dynamited in the quarry to loosen up more rock.

Seeborn said that on May 3, 2007, at about 7:30 a.m. he was awakened by a loud explosion, which he ascertained came from the quarry. He went outside and looked around and was surprised to find several small pieces of granite in his backyard. Further investigation revealed that his basement walls, which were made of 10-inch concrete blocks, were cracked in several places. He obtained several estimates for repairing the wall with the lowest one being $3,250 from Copeland Wall Repair.

On cross-examination by Lester Carter, the lawyer for the defendant company, Seeborn said that he believed the cracked walls had been in good shape before the blast.

Carter asked him if he had any photographs or other evidence to prove that the wall was in good shape before the blast and Seeborn said that he did not.

Carter asked him if what he had told the court was all the evidence he had and Seeborn said that he had retained an engineer who would be called to testify.

The next witness was Charles Acorn who identified himself as a structural engineer. He gave a short resumé of his qualifications. These included a degree in engineering and a association with a firm of engineers for three years. He said he was called by Gordon Seeborn several weeks after the blast to examine the wall and give a report. He read into evidence his report, which he said he personally prepared after his examination of the plaintiff's house. He said he looked at the basement walls on the outside, which he determined were consistently three and one-half feet above ground level. He noticed several places in the exterior, rear basement wall, which showed slight cracks in several other places. There appeared to be cracks or holes, which had been patched with concrete. He said he also examined the walls of the basement inside the house but couldn't find any cracks.

When asked by Carter if he could definitely say the outside cracks were caused by the blast, Acorn said that the odds were 50/50 that they were, but, not having proof of the condition of the wall before the blast, it was difficult to say.

Carter asked him if any windows were broken; Acorn said that there were none at the time of his visit.

When Acorn stepped out of the witness box, Carter stood up quickly to address the court.

He said, "Your Honour, the plaintiff has produced no evidence which would prove that my client caused any cracks in the wall. There was no evidence to prove that the wall was crack-free before the blast. In addition," he said, "and the plaintiff's engineer, Charles Acorn, whose ability I do not question, replied, when I asked him if he could definitely say the cracks were caused by the blast, that the odds were 50/50. In this court the burden of proof is on the plaintiff to prove his case. He has not done so and I would ask Your Honour to dismiss his case."

I asked the plaintiff if he wished to respond to the motion for dismissal made by Carter.

Seeborn said that he felt that he had proven his case and that his engineer had substantiated his evidence.

Before proceeding I must rule on the motion for dismissal. You be the judge.

43

Carol Jamieson

vs.

North West Insurance Co.

Opening Statement

The plaintiff, Carol Jamieson, is suing the defendant, North West Insurance Co., for monies the plaintiff claims are owing under a fire insurance policy. The defendant denies liability.

The Evidence

Jamieson is the owner of a house on the seventh line of Caledon Township. The house was previously occupied by her and is situated at the northeast corner of a 100-acre farm. Jamieson testified that she had lived in the house for about 30 years and that it was previously occupied by her parents for over 60 years.

The house was of frame construction and was reaching a point of some considerable disrepair when the plaintiff built a new bungalow at the extreme southeast corner of the hundred acres. She said that her plan was to have the old house torn down and, indeed, that was a condition of the committee of adjustment in granting the plaintiff a severance and allowing her to build a new bungalow. She was not obliged to demolish the old house until a final inspection of her new house was made by the building inspector. Jamieson said that her new home was probably going to take about four more months to complete, but was livable and she moved in on July 9, 2007.

She testified that, within a week of moving to her new home, Cyrus Small approached her and asked if he could rent the old house for several months. He told the plaintiff that he would pay her $1,200 each month for rent if she would pay the hydro.

Jamieson thought that this was a good deal and gave permission to Small to move in. She said the hydro bill received each month during Small's occupancy was around the same as she had been paying when she lived there.

Delays in the finishing of her new home extended beyond the four months anticipated and Small continued to live in the old frame house. The plaintiff paid the hydro bills, which she said were nothing out of the ordinary.

Jamieson testified that on March 2, 2008, she heard a fire truck pass her home at about three o'clock in the afternoon and when she looked out her window she saw the old frame house engulfed in flames. At that point she said she jumped into her car and drove up the seventh line to the site of the fire where she discovered the farm house had been burned to the ground. Small was nowhere in sight, but his car was gone and the police and fire officials assumed that he had not been killed in the fire.

The plaintiff testified that she was questioned about the fire and her tenant. She said that the insurance adjuster who inspected the burned-out remains indicated to her that, because she was under an obligation to tear the house down shortly, the fire was somewhat suspicious.

Subsequent inspections by a fire marshal indicated that Small was using the house for a "grow-op" for marijuana and that there had been an electrical problem that caused the fire. He also testified that someone had by-passed the hydro meter.

She added that the local police questioned her and told her that they had done a check on her background and that of Small.

Jamieson said that she filed a claim form with her insurance company, the defendant in this action, and her claim was denied.

Having concluded her testimony, Jamieson called as a witness, Constable Jerry Sidal, who indicated that Jamieson had a "clean slate," as he called it, and was not under any suspicion. He did say, however, that Small was well known to the police and had been charged several times with possession of marijuana.

The defendant was represented in court by Angus Reid of the firm of Reid and Kaufman. Reid called Pat Markle, an insurance adjuster representing the defendant, and he testified that the plaintiff's claim was denied because of the use of the house by Small as a grow-op. He said that the use of a house for an illegal purpose nullifies the policy and that the plaintiff should have been aware, as a landlord, of the use to which the house had been put.

Markle was cross-examined by Judy Lessing, Jamieson's lawyer. She asked him how Jamieson could have been aware of the use being made of the house when her hydro bills were quite consistent with her bills for hydro when she lived there. Markle said that probably she would not have been suspicious.

The question to be answered here: whether the insurance company can deny coverage based on the illegal use of the house?

You be the judge.

GEORGE DOWNEY

VS.

ARTHUR ROSS

OPENING STATEMENT

The plaintiff, George Downey, is suing the defendant, Arthur Ross, for conversion of the plaintiff's corn and the defence is that the plaintiff abandoned the corn.

THE EVIDENCE

George Downey testified that he had a 150-acre farm on the first line of Mono in the County of Dufferin. George said that he was primarily a cash crop farmer and that at least 100 acres was planted in corn in 2006 and the balance of his farm was planted in soybeans. He said that the price of corn was about $3.50 a bushel at the time of harvesting in late September and, as it had been a very good growing year, there was an abundance of corn being sold. He decided to sell part of his crop and store 2,000 bushels until the following spring when he anticipated an increase in price.

In March 2007, he sold his farm to Angus Baldwin who allowed him to continue to store his corn on the farm. In September 2008, Angus Baldwin sold the farm to Arthur Ross, the defendant in this action. Downey said that in early

October 2008, he learned that Ross disposed of some of the corn that had rotted and sold the rest to a local grain elevator. The plaintiff said he would be calling as his witness Harvey Potter, who operated the grain elevator.

When Downey finished his testimony, Ross rose to cross-examine him. He asked Downey if he knew the farm had been sold. Downey said that he did, but thought that if Ross wanted the corn removed, he could have asked him to remove it.

The next witness for the plaintiff was Potter. He testified on behalf of the plaintiff and said that when Arthur Ross first talked to him about selling the corn, Ross told him he found it in a storage bin and considered it to have been abandoned by the previous owner. Potter said that he paid Ross $7,500 for the corn.

The defendant then entered the witness box and was sworn in. He admitted that he received $7,500 for the corn, but said he considered the corn to have been abandoned. He said Downey approached him about 10 days after the corn had been removed and taken to Potter's elevator. Downey asked Ross if he knew the corn belonged to him. Ross said he didn't know and it didn't matter because the corn obviously had been there for a while and, as far as he was concerned, it now belonged to him. He said that, when Downey stated he was going to consult with his lawyer, he offered to pay him $3,000 to settle the matter, but Downey refused to accept. The plaintiff waived his right to cross-examine Ross and no further witnesses were called.

The question I have to resolve centres around: what in law is abandonment and what is conversion and which applies in this case?

You be the judge.

JERRY YOUNG, LEGAL REPRESENTATIVE OF
ANDY YOUNG, AND JERRY YOUNG IN HIS
PERSONAL CAPACITY

VS.

CHARLES SNIDER AND SIMCOE HURRICANES
AAA PEEWEE HOCKEY CLUB AND SIMCOE
HURRICANES HOCKEY ASSOCIATION

OPENING STATEMENT

The plaintiff, Jerry Young, is suing the defendants, Charles
Snider, the coach of the Simcoe Hurricanes AAA Peewee
Hockey Club, the Simcoe Hurricanes AAA Peewee
Hockey Club, and the parent association, being the Simcoe
Hurricanes Hockey Association, asking for an order that
his son, Andy, be reinstated to the Simcoe Hurricanes AAA
Peewee Hockey Club.

THE EVIDENCE

Jerry Young took the stand to give evidence on behalf of his
12-year-old son, Andy, and for himself.

Jerry Young said that Andy was kicked off the AAA
Peewee Club. He added that he was banned from the
dressing room about three weeks before Andy was removed

from the team. Jerry said he didn't have any idea why the coach, Charles Snider, asked him to leave the dressing room unless it was because he had several arguments with Snider about the amount of playing time for Andy.

He said his son was an excellent player with superb hockey skills, who had played centre his previous year on an AA team. About two games into the season, Andy was put on defence. Jerry Young said that when he objected, Coach Snider told him that Andy was not fast enough to be a forward. Andy played several more games on defence, before he played three or four games in which he had only about three shifts a game. Finally, he was benched with no playing time.

Jerry said that he spoke with the coach and said his son was a top player on the AA team the year before and he thought the coach was misjudging his abilities. The plaintiff said that the coach told him that Andy was lazy and should transfer back to AA.

According to Jerry, Andy continued to come to practices and dressed for games, but remained on the bench. Young said that he always went to the players' dressing room to help his son do up his skates. The coach said that Andy didn't need help and that Jerry should remain outside as he wanted to give a pep talk to his players. Young said that he refused to leave and there was a verbal exchange between them. The coach told him again to leave and not ever to come in again. Young said he would come in for each game as he didn't trust the coach with Andy. Coach Snider told him he would call the police if Young didn't leave. Several games later, the coach talked to Andy and said that he was wasting his time sitting on the bench and handed him a release so he could play AA.

Jerry was cross-examined by Kevin James, the lawyer representing all the defendants. He asked Jerry how much experience he had coaching AAA hockey. He replied that he had none. James then asked him if he had had any experience coaching hockey or any other sport and, again, Young said that he did not. He then suggested that Young had sworn at the coach in the dressing room with all the players present. Young said that he did not, but admitted that he raised his voice. James said that he had a witness who would testify about his swearing in the dressing room. Young became very agitated and said that he didn't swear and any witness James might have would be lying and they were just trying to get rid of Andy from the team. Kevin James said he had completed his cross-examination and the plaintiff indicated he had no other witnesses.

Kevin James then called Coach Snider to testify. Snider said that, from the very first tryout for the team, Jerry Young was an extremely aggressive parent. He said that Young was constantly yelling at his son from the stands to skate faster, shoot harder, and not to be a pussy cat. He said that other parents at the practices and later at the games moved away from Young as he was loud and rude. The coach said that he had to pick 15 players plus two goalies and that was the number who turned up for the tryouts. He said that hockey had become too expensive a sport for many parents, especially at the AAA level, and it involved a lot of practices and travel for the boys and their parents. He said that out-of-town games sometimes meant the boys had to leave school in mid-afternoon and parents had to take time off work to drive them. Snider said that, if more experienced boys had turned up, Andy would probably not have made the team.

When James asked about Jerry Young's conduct in the dressing room, Snider said that he was frequently cursing and swearing and that it was obvious that Andy was embarrassed by his father's outbursts. Snider also added that he asked Jerry to leave the dressing room on three or four occasions, but Young always said that he would not leave as his son needed him for encouragement and to tie up his skates.

When James asked Snider about offering Andy a release, Snider said that he had and Andy swore at him and said he would rather go back to AA than play for Snider. Snider said that he couldn't believe the foul language that Andy used. He said that never before had he been bad-mouthed by a player.

According to Snider, when Andy left the dressing room in tears, his father burst in and swore at the coach and called him some very foul names. At that time the assistant coach, the trainer, and seven or eight players were in the dressing room. Snider told him to leave the dressing room and Jerry came over and pushed him and swore again before he left.

Jerry Young proceeded with his cross-examination of Coach Snider. He asked Snider if he had any children who showed promise as hockey players. James was quick in objecting and said that this case was about Young and not about the other members of the team. I ruled in favour of James's objection and told the plaintiff to proceed without any further personalities.

Young then asked Snider what qualifications he had as a coach and Snider replied that he had coached minor hockey at the house league level for six years and had been coaching AAA for four years. Young said that he heard that Snider had been having trouble with players and parents for several years. Snider was quick to deny this and said that Young and his son were the only persons he encountered who were rude and abusive. He added that some parents thought their kids should get more ice time, but that he was the coach and in this competitive league he had to play players that would produce so the team could win. He added that this was not house league hockey where winning was nice, but not the prime goal. He said that in AAA the players were keen to win and the purpose of the AAA and the Simcoe Hurricanes Hockey Association was to develop players and to win hockey games. Young asked him if he didn't think Andy would be one of these players and Snider quickly responded that he thought Andy was a nice kid up until the time he swore at him, but that Andy lacked the talent and the desire necessary to be playing AAA hockey.

The next witness for the defence was Greg Clarkson, the president of the Simcoe Hurricanes Hockey Association. James asked him how the coaches were chosen. He replied that they must have at least three years coaching house league or rep hockey and have some positive results and feedback from parents. He added that a police check was done on prospective coaches and that AAA coaches must take a comprehensive course that involved hockey skills and psychology. He said that Snider passed the coaching course with flying colours.

Jerry Young then had his chance to cross-examine Clarkson. His only question was why the association didn't keep an eye on Snider as he was obviously a "lousy" coach.

I warned Young that he could ask questions, but not to make speeches.

Clarkson then replied that at least four times during the hockey season, someone from the association office would sit in on a game to confirm the coaches were coaching as they were supposed to. He added that, until Andy had been released, Snider had been checked on twice by the association and that the association was happy with the way Snider was performing.

James said that he had no other witnesses and that the Simcoe Hurricanes AAA Peewee Hockey Club was under the control of the association and there would be nothing they could add to Clarkson's evidence.

The questions I have to decide: whether Andy Young was unjustly removed from the Simcoe Hurricanes AAA Peewee Hockey Club and whether the coach was justified in removing Jerry Young from the change room?

You be the judge.

RAVI AND NORIDA SALIB

VS.

KAPOOR SANDEEN

OPENING STATEMENT

The plaintiffs, Ravi and Norida Salib, are suing the defendant, Kapoor Sandeen, for $6,500, being the monies they paid the defendant on a contract to take pictures at their wedding on June 15, 2008.

THE EVIDENCE

Ravi Salib was the first person to testify. He said that he and Norida, who was then his fiancée, were planning a lavish Indian wedding and wished to have extensive photo coverage. The wedding ceremony and the following banquet and festivities would take place over a 14-hour period. They spoke with some Indian friends who had similar large weddings and their friends recommended the defendant as an excellent photographer. They were shown the albums and videos of the friends' weddings and were excited by the quality and number of shots Kapoor Sandeen produced. They went to the defendant's studio and suggested what they wanted, which included several small albums of about 50 pictures each to send to their grandparents in India. Sandeen said that he would produce a video of the ceremony to be played during the banquet to follow the ceremony and would take approximately 500 shots from which they could chose 300 for their own album. The total cost would be $6,500, which was within their budget, and they immediately retained Sandeen, signed a contract, and paid in full his fee of $6,500. They were pleased to have retained a photographer who was himself Indian and was familiar with Indian weddings.

Ravi testified that, on the day of the wedding, Kapoor arrived on time with one assistant and many photos were taken during the actual ceremony. The wedding banquet was in another location in a Brampton hotel. Sandeen was highly visible throughout the day taking pictures and he told Ravi that his assistant had gone back to the studio to put the video presentation together.

During the wedding feast that followed, Ravi was furious to find that, after about every three or four pictures on the video presentation, there was an advertisement promoting the defendant's studio. When the plaintiff complained to the defendant, he was advised that it couldn't be changed and so the video with the commercials continued throughout the banquet and dance.

Ravi said that that was as much evidence as he wished to give and that his wife, Norida, would tell the rest of the story.

The defendant indicated that he did not want to question Ravi.

Norida took the stand, was sworn in, and began her testimony. She started by saying she confirmed all of her husband's testimony. Then she began a chronology of events after the wedding.

First, she said she phoned the defendant after she and Ravi returned from their honeymoon. She looked at her notes and said that call was on July 3. The receptionist at the defendant's studio said that she would have him call.

He never did return her call. She phoned on three more occasions in July: July 5, July 8, and July 17. She said that on all occasions the receptionist said Kapoor was out, but she would have him call.

On July 20, after discussing her frustration with Ravi, they decided to drive to his studio in Mississauga. On entering the reception area they were stunned to see a poster, which was estimated at 30 inches by 18 inches, showing a picture of them embracing with a caption "Specialist in Indian Weddings." After they had been waiting for about an hour, Kapoor came out of his office and greeted them like they were long lost friends. Ravi asked Kapoor why their picture was on the wall in the reception area and he responded that he didn't think they would mind. Norida said that she told him that they did mind and to take it down.

When she asked about their proofs of the wedding pictures, he said that he had been very busy, but would get at it the next day. She said that she was really upset that the small albums for their grandparents in India had not been started and told Kapoor that her grandparents were old and not well and it would be nice if they saw the pictures before they died. Kapoor said that he would work on the small albums first and that the plaintiffs could come back in five days to pick the pictures from the proofs to put into the small albums.

On the drive home Ravi said that if Kapoor had enough nerve to put up a poster of them in his reception area, they should check his website to see if they were featured there. Upon arrival at home Norida testified that she went straight to the computer and googled Kapoor's website. She said that she found, to their total amazement, several pictures of them, and Kapoor was again promoting Indian weddings. Norida said that her husband phoned Kapoor who, by some miracle, answered the phone, and Ravi told him to get their pictures off his website. She said that the pictures were gone the next day.

Norida said that on July 29 she phoned Kapoor's studio and said they were coming to pick up the proofs. The receptionist said that she would check with Kapoor and phone her back. On July 31 the receptionist phoned and said that the proofs were not yet ready, but Kapoor said that they would be ready on August 10. According to the receptionist, Lynne Sandeen, Kapoor was extremely busy with at least two weddings every weekend.

On August 10, the plaintiffs went to the studio and Kapoor produced around 50 proofs for them to approve or reject. Norida said that she and Ravi went through the proofs and picked 26 for the small albums. At this point Ravi told Kapoor that, unless they got the remaining proofs by August 20, they would be seeking legal advice.

Norida said that August 20 came and went and no word was received by Kapoor. On August 22, Norida said that she phoned her lawyer, Mohamed Khan, to get an appointment and she was advised that the lawyer was in India on vacation and wouldn't be back until September 15. She made an appointment for September 16.

He said that before taking action he would write a letter to Kapoor threatening legal action unless he produced all the proofs by September 30.

No proofs were received by the plaintiffs or Khan by October 4, but Kapoor phoned and said that he didn't appreciate being threatened by a lawyer. Norida said that she then phoned Khan and told him to proceed with the action. Sandeen was served with the claim in this action on October 22 and he filed a defence on November 8. Norida said that, as of today, December 18, they have seen no proofs other than those chosen for the small albums for the grandparents.

Norida was then cross-examined by the defendant. He asked her if she knew anything about the process of taking and developing photographs. She replied that she did not, but, as he was paid $6,500, she thought he would have been more professional. He asked if she still wanted the photos and she replied that she did, but, as he had put them to so much grief and agony, she thought the price should be reduced or, better still, that their money should be refunded.

The defendant then entered the witness box and was sworn in. He said that the Salibs were a pushy and irritating couple who were never satisfied with anything he did. he said that he was extremely busy and the Salibs stressed him out. He said that he had the proofs with him and was prepared to turn them over today and let the Salibs contact another photographer to finish up his work. He added that he would refund $2,000 of their money to them.

I asked the plaintiffs if they were prepared to accept his offer to settle and we took a short recess so they could discuss the offer.

When the court resumed in about 30 minutes, Ravi Salib said that he and his wife had looked over the proofs, talked to Kapoor and agreed to accept the proofs provided they did not have a stamp on them saying they were proofs and the property of Kapoor. Kapoor said he agreed to this proposal and that they would have the unmarked proofs tomorrow, and Kapoor was agreeable to returning $3,500 to them.

The defendant confirmed this arrangement and I asked about court costs. Ravi said that they would each absorb their own court costs.

You be the judge.

Larson August

vs.

Carl James, Carrying on Business as Carl's Dry Cleaning

Opening Statement

The plaintiff, Larson August, is suing the defendant, Carl James, for $855 for loss of a suit taken to the defendant's place of business for dry cleaning.

The Evidence

August testified under oath that he took his "Sunday-best suit" to Carl's Dry Cleaning to have it dry cleaned. He said he had been using Carl's services for eight or nine years and that he had always been quite satisfied with his service. On leaving the suit, he advised the defendant that he was going away on holidays and that he would pick it up in two weeks. When he returned from vacation, he found to his surprise that the store in the strip mall where Carl had his business was totally gutted by a fire. There was a sign on the door advising customers that anything they had left for cleaning was destroyed and that he would not be opening for business again.

The plaintiff made some inquiries and discovered that Carl was working for another cleaning establishment about three blocks away. August went to Carl's place of employment and asked him about replacing his suit through insurance. Carl refused to talk to him. At this point the plaintiff commenced action.

The defendant, Carl James, entered the witness box and was sworn in. He said that he recalled August and his suit, but that all customers are given a copy of an order form indicating what they have left for cleaning and the date the item would be ready for pickup. James entered into evidence a copy of the order form and read the waiver form printed on the back. The waiver read: "Carl's Dry Cleaning assumes no responsibility for loss or damage to the items listed on the reverse side of this form, including loss or damage by flood, explosion, fire, or Acts of God."

He said that this clause exonerated him from all responsibility for the plaintiff's loss.

When cross-examined by the plaintiff's lawyer, Cyril Lawson, James admitted that he had insurance for liability and fire, but he said that, for some reason, the insurance company was delaying payment. He added that he didn't expect to be paid as a result of the fire. Lawson continued with this line of questioning and asked pointedly whether the insurance company suspected that the fire was suspicious. Jones admitted that it did. He also admitted that had he received a settlement from the insurance company, he would have been able to pay for all or part of his customers' losses. When asked by Lawson if he pointed out the waiver clause to August or had him sign, he indicated that he had not.

The questions to be answered in this case: whether the waiver exonerates the defendant from liability and, even if it does, should the defendant still pay the plaintiff for his loss?

You be the judge.

DR. JOSEPH RYAN

VS.

CLARE INNES

OPENING STATEMENT

In this action, the plaintiff, Dr. Ryan, is suing for $893, being his account for dental services, and the defendant, Clare Innes, has a claim for $400, being the deposit he paid to Dr. Ryan.

THE EVIDENCE

Dr. Ryan entered the witness box and explained his position. He said that the defendant had been a patient of his for three and a half years during which time he had some major fillings and the usual six-month checkup and cleaning. He reviewed his patient's chart and indicated that Innes had always paid for services rendered on leaving the dental office.

At his last appointment for a cleaning and checkup on June 3, 2007, an X-ray was taken and it disclosed serious decay in the lower left rear molar. Dr. Ryan said that he advised Innes that he would probably have trouble with the tooth soon, if some remedial steps were not taken. At that point Clare indicated to Dr. Ryan that the tooth had been sore for several months and that he had taken Tylenol to ease the pain. Innes told the plaintiff that he had not divulged the problem as he couldn't stand having dental work done. He then asked Dr. Ryan what could be done and Dr. Ryan advised him that he had two options; he could have the tooth extracted or he could have a root canal, which would save the tooth. Dr. Ryan quoted him the price of both procedures. The extraction would cost $250 unless he ran into serious difficulties, and then the cost could run as high as $450. If Innes opted for the root canal, the cost would be $1,200 or slightly less if it was not necessary to use the usual amount of anaesthetic.

Dr. Ryan said that Innes did not want to lose the tooth, so he said that he wanted to go ahead with the root canal. A deposit of $400 was requested by the dental assistant and an appointment was made for June 10. The deposit was paid by Innes.

On June 10, Innes appeared at the office of Dr. Ryan and, before any work was commenced, Innes said he could not pay immediately but would like to pay in two instalments over a two-month period. The plaintiff agreed with this arrangement and said that he only did so because of Innes's good payment record.

The root canal was completed over two appointments. The first was the drilling and cleaning out of the decayed tooth and packing with antibiotics. During the second appointment, the balance of the procedure was completed. Dr. Ryan said that Clare seemed to be happy with the results and, in fact, dropped into the office about 10 days later and told the receptionist that he had done a good job. Dr. Ryan said that he would call the receptionist as a witness, to confirm that conversation, if necessary.

To speed up the trial I asked Innes if he would confirm the conversation to save calling the receptionist to testify and he said that there was never any such conversation. I advised Dr. Ryan that, as the conversation was hearsay, he should call his receptionist.

Dr. Ryan said that reminders of overdue accounts were routinely sent out around the 15th of each month. Reminders were sent out to the defendant on July 15, August 18, and September 16. The plaintiff said that he personally called Innes on October 8 to enquire about his overdue account. Dr. Ryan said that the defendant told him that he had done "a lousy job" and would be paying nothing.

The plaintiff then produced affidavits from two other dentists, namely Sally Wrightman and George Bower. Both affidavits set out the usual procedure in doing a root canal. I asked Innes if he had seen these affidavits and he confirmed that he had. I also asked him if he chose not to subpoena these two dentists so that he could question them on their affidavits and he responded that he considered all dentists to be, and I quote, "money grabbing mechanics," and he didn't want to have any dealings with any of them. Both affidavits were read into evidence by Dr. Ryan. The affidavit of Dr. Wrightman was especially interesting as she indicated that she had practised for three years with Dr. Ryan before opening up her own practice. She said that she had assisted Dr. Ryan perhaps 30 to 35 times doing root canals and she had absolute confidence in Dr. Ryan's ability to perform the procedure. Both dentists indicated that the prices for Dr. Ryan's services were well within the range charged by themselves and by other dentists they talked to.

When Dr. Ryan completed his evidence, Innes chose to cross-examine him. Innes started out by saying that Dr. Ryan was an incompetent dentist and overcharged his patients. I had to stop him with his speech and to remind him that cross-examination was his opportunity to ask questions about Dr. Ryan's evidence. The defendant asked Dr. Ryan how long he had practised. The answer was 17 years. He then asked how many root canals he had done and Dr. Ryan said that he didn't know exactly, but said on an average, he did about one a week, so he thought at least 600 to 700 over his career in dentistry.

Innes asked about the alleged conversation with the receptionist at which time he was supposed to have said what a good job the dentist had done. I pointed out what I had already said about that conversation being hearsay and it was not, at this point in time, admissible evidence. I said that, if Dr. Ryan wanted to call the receptionist to give testimony, Innes would have a chance to cross-examine her.

Innes then said he had nothing more to say and sat down.

Dr. Ryan then called his receptionist to the stand. She was sworn in and advised the court that her name was Emily Parrotski and that she had worked for Dr. Ryan for about six years.

When Dr. Ryan asked her if she had a conversation with Innes after his surgery, she responded that he did drop into the office about 10 days after the surgery and said that Dr. Ryan was a great dentist and that he was very happy with the results of his root canal.

Innes, in cross-examination, asked her if she was positive if it was he who came in and she said yes. He asked if he appeared to be under the influence of alcohol and Emily said that she couldn't say for sure, but that Innes seemed to be sober and that she couldn't smell anything on his breath. Innes reminded her that she was under oath and Emily said that she would never lie about such a serious matter.

Innes then was sworn in and began to tell his story. He said that he really wanted his tooth pulled and that he couldn't afford a root canal. He said that Dr. Ryan had not given him an adequate amount of freezing and he was in considerable pain throughout the procedure. He added that his tooth continued to ache. He said that he didn't recall talking to Emily and that he had a drinking problem and was probably drunk if he did come to the office.

The defendant said he talked to another dentist, named Josh Silverstein, about the work of Dr. Ryan, but that the other dentist declined to come to court to support Innes's position unless he was paid and only after a thorough examination and an X-ray. The defendant said that he wanted his $400 deposit back and denied that he had asked for time to pay, saying the $400 was to be the total cost for an extraction.

Dr. Ryan then proceeded to cross-examine Innes. He asked if Innes was aware that he was given a receipt for the $400 that specified that it was a deposit on a root canal with the balance payable over a two-month period. Innes said that he never got such a receipt. Ryan then asked him why he didn't subpoena the other dentist to come to court to support his case. Innes replied that the dentist whom he consulted wanted $200 per hour to attend and he couldn't afford it.

When I asked Dr. Ryan if he wanted to testify in regards to Innes' claim for $400, he said that he believed the evidence of all parties so far substantiated his claim for $893 and that the defendant's claim for $400 was totally bogus.

The questions to be decided here: did Innes contract to have a root canal, was Dr. Ryan's account reasonable, and should Clare Innes get his $400 deposit back?

You be the judge.

ANDREW AND CHRISTINE BARKLY

VS.

VACATIONS IN THE SUN LTD.

OPENING STATEMENT

The plaintiffs, Andrew and Christine Barkly, are suing the defendant, Vacations in the Sun Ltd., for return of monies for a trip to French Guiana, the cost of returning home, plus other expenses.

THE EVIDENCE

Andrew Barkly testified under oath that he was looking for an all-inclusive holiday to French Guiana. His travel agent, Cathy of Get-a-Way Travel, from whom he had purchased many trips, showed him a brochure by the defendant company. He said that Cathy did not know about the defendant, but that their brochure painted a glowing picture of a resort in French Guiana, called Guiana Tropical Resort.

Andrew took the information home to his wife, and they decided it looked like a really nice place and the price was within their budget.

Andrew had a copy of the brochure, which he entered into evidence and read some parts of it. It was an all-inclusive resort hotel on the beach. Small sailboats were to be included, as well as snorkelling equipment and a boat ride to the best area to snorkel. The hotel was newly completed about three months before the date in the brochure. It had two restaurants. One was a buffet-type restaurant and the other a more formal dining room with free wine and drinks in both locations.

The Barklys paid the travel agent $3,600 for the 10-day stay.

Andrew told the court that, when they arrived at the hotel, they were shown to their fourth-storey room by the porter. When they looked into the bathroom, they discovered there was no toilet seat and the shower had no shower head. Andrew tried to phone down to the front desk without success. Apparently the phones had not yet been connected. He went down to the front desk and complained about the room and was told by the clerk that there were no other rooms available. When he asked for a reservation for dinner, he was told that the restaurants were not yet open because of a plumbers' strike. The clerk suggested two alternative restaurants further down the beach, but she indicated that the plaintiffs would have to take a taxi to get to them as they were six and four miles away. At this point Christine Barkly appeared in the lobby and, when Andrew told her of the eating arrangements, she burst into tears and said that she wanted to go home. Andrew said that he used the phone at reception to get in touch with the airline that had brought them down from Toronto by way of Miami. He was told they could get seats on the next flight back to Miami, which would be in two days, but they couldn't get out of Miami for at least four days.

Andrew said that he arranged flights and told the hotel clerk they were leaving the next day and would expect a total refund of their $3,600, plus the cost of their meals and accommodation in Miami. He said that the clerk said it was out of her hands and she couldn't give a refund.

Andrew said that he and Christine took a taxi to the closest restaurant where their meal cost US$47.25. He said that she knew more about their expenses and she would testify next.

Gordon Davis, the lawyer for the defendant, suggested that his client was unaware of the situation at the hotel and asked Andrew if he had considered suing the travel agent. Andrew replied that the package was advertised by Vacations in the Sun and he didn't see why he should look elsewhere for compensation. Davis asked him if he had received an offer from the defendant to settle the lawsuit. Andrew replied that he did receive an offer, but it was totally unsatisfactory.

Christine Barkly was sworn in as a witness and said that she agreed completely with her husband's testimony. She said that she had a list of their out-of-pocket expenses that included the taxi and dinner down the road from the hotel, a taxi to and from the hotel in Miami, and meals in Miami. These additional items totalled US$635.13.

Davis did not cross-examine Christine on her evidence

The matter to be decided: whether the Barklys are entitled to a refund of $3,600 for their trip, plus their expenses?

You be the judge.

FRED JONES, CARRYING ON BUSINESS AS JONES BUTCHER SHOP

VS.

JASON MCKAY

OPENING STATEMENT

The plaintiff, Fred Jones, is suing the defendant, Jason McKay, for $6,500, being the alleged loss of business caused by the failure of Jason McKay to supply hogs to the plaintiff.

THE EVIDENCE

Fred Jones is a butcher and has a store known as Jones Butcher Shop and Jason McKay is a farmer in the hog business.

The plaintiff testified that he has a flourishing butcher shop and that, for the previous four years, he was supplied by the defendant with 40 to 50 hogs a year as requested by him. He said that the demand for a half pig was increasing greatly by his customers since the price of beef was escalating and the price of pork was dropping.

Jones said that, when some customers wanted pork, he would give McKay the order, pay him and McKay would have the pigs slaughtered and delivered to Jones's shop for butchering and packaging.

To secure a steady supply for the increasing pork sales at his shop, Jones said that he entered into an oral contract with McKay to supply on request 50 hogs each year. The cost per hog was established at a fixed price of 50 cents a pound. The agreement was to run for four years.

The plaintiff said that, for approximately two years, the dealings between him and McKay went extremely well, but in the winter of 2007 McKay had a barn fire. His total inventory of hogs was destroyed so that he could no longer supply Jones.

Jason McKay testified that he and Jones had a good working relationship and he was sure both benefited financially. He said that during an electrical storm his hog barn was hit by lightning, a fire started and his barn and 300 hogs were destroyed.

The defendant said that it would take at least three years to get his business up and running again. He said that he knew Jones was disappointed and inconvenienced; he admitted that the price of hogs had increased and that Jones would have to pay more.

The question to be decided: whether there was a binding contract and, if so, should McKay reimburse Jones for the extra amount he had to pay for hogs?

You be the judge.

MARY ELIZABETH CLARK

VS.

JACK JORDAN, CARRYING ON BUSINESS AS JORDAN GOLDEN RETRIEVER KENNELS

OPENING STATEMENT

The plaintiff, Mary Elizabeth Clark, is suing the defendant, Jack Jordan, for $1,200, being the cost of a dog named Fred, purchased by the plaintiff from the defendant.

THE EVIDENCE

Mary Elizabeth Clark testified that she did a considerable amount of research through the Canadian Kennel Club and on the Internet to find a reliable and recommended kennel specializing in golden retrievers. She also tracked down and interviewed several other owners of golden retrievers purchased from Jordan and received glowing reports about the defendant and his dogs.

Clark said that she was told by Jordan that Fred had received his shots and that the dog, which was seven weeks old when Clark first saw him, was a "picture of health" and was ready to find a suitable home. The plaintiff gave Jordan a cheque for $1,200.

There is no dispute that Clark paid Jordan $1,200 for

Fred and that, on July 2, 2008, she took Fred to her home.

Clark further testified that within a week Fred had a seizure which lasted about 30 minutes. She phoned her veterinarian, Dr. Amy Snider, who told her that, if it happened again, she should bring Fred in and have him checked out and get some pills to reduce the likelihood of further seizures.

Clark said that she phoned Jordan to put him on notice of the problem. She said that Jordan told her there was no guarantee on the purchase of a dog. During the next two and a half weeks, Fred had a seizure about every second or third day. After the second seizure, Clark took Fred to Dr. Snider.

Snider was called as a witness for Clark. Snider indicated that she was a practising veterinarian, having graduated from the Ontario Veterinary College 12 years before this trial. She testified that tests she performed on Fred indicated that he was likely to have seizures for the rest of his life. She also said that Fred had a seizure while in her office and that she injected a tranquilizer to bring him out of it.

Snider also testified, on being asked by Clark's lawyer, that she had at least six kennel owners as clients and regularly gave their dogs their puppy shots. She said that most of them would take back a sick dog and refund the purchase price.

Jordan did not take the opportunity to cross-examine Dr. Snider on this point.

In his testimony, Jordan said that Fred was the mutt of the litter, but that he had had no seizures while in his care. He said that the plaintiff asked him to take back Fred and refund his money, but he refused. When cross-examined by the lawyer for Clark, he admitted that on occasion a dog will have seizures. He also testified that his kennel was approved by the Kennel Club of Canada.

When Clark's lawyer suggested that it might be prudent to take Fred back and avoid any unnecessary publicity, he said that he didn't care and that he was prepared to rely on his reputation as a first-class breeder. He also said that Clark should have had her veterinarian examine Fred before she paid for him.

Jordan also said that he would not take Fred back and replace him with another dog.

The question I have to decide: whether the plaintiff should have her $1,200 refunded? I note that she has not asked for reimbursement of her vet bills.

You be the judge.

52

JANICE SIMPSON

VS.

CALEDON HILLS RENTALS INC., AND CALEDON HILLS RENTALS INC. VS. GEORGE NASH AND AUDREY PORTER

OPENING STATEMENT

This action was originally two actions which, on motion to this court by Caledon Hills Rentals Inc. for a consolidation of actions, was ordered to be tried as one action. The circumstances in both actions arise out of the same situation. Janice Simpson is suing Caledon Hills Rentals Inc. for $2,000 for inconvenience and out-of-pocket expenses in regard to the rental of an apartment owned by Caledon Hills. Caledon Hills had in effect third partied George Nash, a tenant in the apartment Janice Simpson believed she had rented, and Caledon Hills is also suing Audrey Porter, the superintendent of the apartment building.

THE EVIDENCE

Janice Simpson testified that she saw a sign on the lawn of 70 Cranberry Court in Caledon indicating that there was a two-bedroom apartment for rent. She said that she made enquiries about the apartment from the superintendent, Audrey Porter, whose phone number appeared on the sign. After viewing the apartment, Simpson completed an application form and left Porter with a deposit equal to one month's rent. She completed the application on May 28, 2008, and was told by Porter that the apartment would be available on July 1. She said that the owner of the apartment building, Caledon Hills Rentals, accepted her application on May 29.

Simpson said that upon acceptance of her application she gave a notice to the manager of the women's shelter where she had been living for about three weeks that she would be leaving on July 1. She started packing up her belongings and hired a moving truck for 7:00 a.m. on July 1. On July 1 she arrived along with the moving truck at 70 Cranberry Court where she was met by Porter.

Janice said that Porter told her that she had just checked with the tenants in the apartment Simpson had rented to determine when the tenants would be leaving. The tenants told Porter that they were not vacating until August 1.

Simpson testified that she took it upon herself to talk to the tenants, whose name she could not recall, and asked at what time they would be leaving. She said that they told her that they had no intention of leaving until August 1. When she told them that she had rented the apartment as of July 1, the man slammed the door in her face.

The plaintiff, at this point, said that she was very upset and told the superintendent that she wanted to talk to the owner of the apartment building. Simpson said that Audrey Porter did call someone, whom she identified as Howard, and explained to him what was happening and asked him to come down to the apartment. Meanwhile, Simpson and her truck waited on the road.

Simpson said that when Howard arrived, she and Porter met him and explained the situation. She said that Howard went to the apartment that was to be vacated, came back in a few minutes and confirmed that the existing tenant had no intention of moving. Howard said that the tenant showed him a copy of his "Notice to Vacate," which he apparently gave to Porter. The notice clearly indicated that the tenant was not moving until August 1.

At this point Howard said that he would try to find the plaintiff another apartment and he left, supposedly, to make some enquiries about available places. Simpson said that he returned in about an hour and said that he had located another apartment into which she could move immediately. She went to look at the apartment and came back in about half an hour. She said that the apartment was a "disgusting dump," and she refused to take it. The plaintiff said that she phoned the shelter where she had been staying and they agreed to let her stay until August 1.

Simpson said that she wanted to be reimbursed for the cost of her moving truck and storage for one month of her belongings and something for her stress and inconvenience. She produced a bill for the truck rental, but she paid nothing to store her belongings as they were left in a friend's garage for free.

The next party to give testimony was Howard, who identified himself as Howard Smada, the sole owner of Caledon Hills Rentals.

Smada said that he sympathized with Simpson's position, but felt the problem had been satisfactorily resolved when Simpson was allowed to go back to the shelter. He said that he had already given Simpson $400 to compensate her for rental of her moving truck.

Smada said that he accepted Simpson's application to rent the apartment based on information his superintendent, Audrey Porter, had provided indicating that George Nash was moving out July 1. He also said that, when he asked

Porter for the notice to vacate that Nash had given her, she could not find it.

Smada told the court that he felt that the whole mess was caused by the incompetence of Audrey Porter in not reading Nash's notice to vacate and in advising Janice Simpson that the apartment would be available on July 1.

As the owner of Caledon Hills Rentals, Smada said that he realized that George Nash was not at fault and he was prepared to drop Caledon's action against him. He also stated that Nash had, in any event, not filed a defence so had not incurred any costs.

Smada said that, if the court found Caledon Hills responsible in any way to Simpson, the company should be reimbursed by Porter.

When Audrey Porter took the stand, she testified that she honestly believed that Nash was moving out on July 1 and she acted in good faith in renting the apartment to Simpson.

On cross-examination by Smada, Porter denied destroying Nash's notice to vacate. She also said that she thought it was not her responsibility to keep dates straight and that that was up to Smada, the landlord.

The question to be decided: who, if anyone, is responsible to Janice Simpson for the inconvenience and expenses she suffered?

You be the judge.

53

CLARE SNEDDON

VS.

GEORGE ANDERSON

OPENING STATEMENT

The plaintiff, Clare Sneddon, is suing the defendant, George Anderson, for $8,500 plus costs for unlawfully cutting trees from the plaintiff's property.

THE EVIDENCE

The plaintiff and the defendant are adjoining landowners of summer cottage property on Lake of Bays in Muskoka.

The plaintiff testified that he purchased his property in 1973 and at that time Anderson owned the adjoining property to the north. He said that his property was 200 feet wide by a depth of approximately 950 feet, and ran from the access road to the lake. The property was heavily wooded with hemlock, oak, maple, and beech trees, most of which were at least 23 inches in diameter. Anderson's property was 100 feet wide and of the same depth. The plaintiff said that Anderson's property was less dense with trees as several cuttings had been made over the last 15 years and, in addition, the defendant had widened his access lane, resulting in the removal of many birch, hemlock, and ash trees.

Sneddon indicated that, in the winter or early spring before he arrived to open up his cottage for the summer season, a number of trees that appeared to be on his property had been cut down and removed, leaving stumps of between two and three feet. He said that he last attended his cottage in mid-December to shovel the snow off his roof and, at that time there was no evidence of tree removal.

The plaintiff phoned the defendant to ask about the tree removal and the defendant stated that all the trees that he had removed were on his property. According to the plaintiff, Anderson refused to discuss the matter further. Sneddon thought Anderson's attitude to be somewhat defensive, particularly when they had been friendly neighbours for over 35 years.

Sneddon said his next step was to find the survey stakes that were planted when he had the property surveyed in 1973. The only stakes he could find were one at the road and one at the lake. As the area had dense growth and was rocky and rough, he was unable to determine exactly where the lot line was.

The plaintiff said that his next step was to call in a surveyor to stake the lot line between his property and that of the defendant. The survey was completed in about three weeks with stakes marking the line planted every 125 feet apart. The plaintiff produced the new survey in evidence as well as the surveyor's bill of $1,600.

Sneddon was then able to determine that 37 trees on his property had been removed.

Sneddon said that he called Anderson again and advised him of the survey and the cut trees. Anderson, at this point, said that if any of Sneddon's trees were removed, it was the logger's fault, as Anderson had told him where the lot line was located. Sneddon testified that Anderson refused to discuss any compensation for his loss.

According to Sneddon his next step was to retain the services of an arborist to determine the value of the trees that had been removed from his property.

The next witness was Geoff Wozniak, who said that he had a degree in forestry and a certificate as a certified arborist. He said that he had examined over 400 bush sites in his five years of practice and had testified in over 30 cases involving circumstances similar to Sneddon's. Wozniak testified that the cut trees ranged from 23 to 32 inches in diameter and that, based on the diameter, he was able to determine how high the trees would have been. He also stated that, based on his calculations, a logger would have paid between $8,300 and $8,500 for the trees.

The defendant took the witness stand and said that he couldn't dispute the arborist's testimony, but said that he instructed the logger where the lot line was. If anyone was responsible, it was the logger, and Sneddon should have sued him.

Anderson was then cross-examined by the plaintiff. Sneddon asked him how he was able to determine the lot line between their respective properties. Anderson said that he remembered where the stakes had been placed for the 1973 survey. Sneddon suggested that there had been much growth over the last 35 years and wondered how Anderson was so sure. He replied that he had a very good memory and a photographic mind. Sneddon responded that, if his memory was good, how come the new survey proved him to be wrong about the lot line. Anderson did not respond.

Sneddon then asked him how much he received from the logger and he replied that it was none of Sneddon's business. Sneddon did not pursue the matter further.

Sneddon also asked him if he was prepared to make an offer to settle and he responded again that it was not his fault and that Sneddon should have sued the logger.

When I asked the parties if they would like a recess of 15 minutes to discuss settlement, the plaintiff said that he was willing to talk to the defendant. The defendant said that there was nothing to talk about and that Sneddon should have sued the logger.

The issue to be decided: whether responsibility for cutting the trees belongs to the defendant or to the logger?

You be the judge.

54

LINDA SNELGROVE

VS.

CARMAN FREDERICO

OPENING STATEMENT

The plaintiff, Linda Snelgrove, is suing the defendant, Carman Frederico, for $2,300 and costs in regard to a purchase of a house. The plaintiff's claim is for $1,100 for a new refrigerator and $1,200 to repair a fence.

THE EVIDENCE

The plaintiff entered into an agreement of purchase and sale of a residential home at 13 Carberry Road in Brampton. The vendor of the property was the defendant. The agreement was signed and accepted on April 16. The closing date was to be April 30. The plaintiff testified that, when she looked at the house, there were two refrigerators that appeared to be working. One was in the kitchen and one in the basement. Both were included in the agreement. When the transaction closed on April 30, she found out that the basement refrigerator was not working. She also said that a fence in the backyard, separating the subject property from the neighbour directly behind, was broken between two four-by-four posts that were approximately eight feet apart.

In the agreement there was a clause similar to ones seen in many house purchase contracts indicating that the offer was conditional until May 10 upon the purchaser having a satisfactory house inspection done. This is slightly strange as the closing date was before the inspection date deadline.

When cross-examined by the defendant's lawyer, Oscar Wildman, the plaintiff said that she, in fact, didn't have an inspection done. She indicated that the real estate agent approached her to change the date of the inspection to April 20. She admitted that she told the agent to forget the inspection as she felt there was insufficient time to have it done and she agreed to sign a waiver of her right to have the inspection. She admitted that she did sign the waiver.

Wildman asked Snelgrove how many times she had viewed the property after the contract was agreed and she said three times. She said that once was to measure the curtains and the next two times were just to see the house and yard. Wildman asked her if she checked out the basement refrigerator and she admitted she hadn't. When he asked her about the broken fence, she admitted that, when she first saw it, she thought the section of fence in question had a slight lean to it, but that it was not broken down like it was when the deal closed.

Wildman produced a photo of the fence and asked Snelgrove if she had been given a copy and she admitted she had. She looked at the picture and said that it must have been taken long before the deal closed.

Wildman then called his client, Carman Frederico, to testify and she was duly sworn in by the court clerk. Frederico said that the refrigerator in the basement had not been working for years. She said that, when they moved into the house about 15 years ago, she bought a new refrigerator and had the movers take the old kitchen refrigerator to the basement. Her husband kept his beer in it until it quit about six years ago. Wildman asked her why she didn't dispose of the basement refrigerator and she responded that since they moved in some structural changes had been made to the stairway in the basement and her husband and son determined that it couldn't be taken up the stairs.

The lawyer then again referred to the picture of the fence and asked the defendant to identify it. She said that it was a picture she took on April 2 when the house was listed with the real estate agent. Wildman asked why she bothered to take a picture of the fence and she responded that the real estate agent suggested that it might be a good idea in case a purchaser later came along and said it didn't have a lean on it when they viewed the property. And she added it was a good idea as that was exactly what happened in this case.

Wildman then addressed the court and asked for a dismissal of the plaintiff's case. I denied his motion and told him that I was prepared to give my judgment when all the evidence had been presented. Both parties indicated they were done with their evidence.

The question to be decided: whether the plaintiff has proven her case as the onus was on her on the balance of probabilities to convince me that I should rule in her favour?

You be the judge.

PART II

THE
JUDGMENTS

LYNNE SMITH

VS.

GERALD BROWN

JUDGE ADAMS'S DECISION

I accept the evidence of Lynne that it was Gerald who called off the wedding.

When Lynne and Gerald became engaged, a contract was created. The essential ingredients of a contract are an offer, an acceptance of the offer, and some consideration. By Gerald proposing marriage, he made an offer to Lynne that she accepted. The consideration was the ring given by the offerer, Gerald, to the offeree, Lynne.

As in any business transaction if the person making the deposit (the ring) withdraws from the transaction, he loses his deposit.

Lynne shall have the ring and $3,775 for her expenses and any court costs that she has incurred in bringing this matter to trial.

James Karston

vs.

The Plumbing Place

Judge Adams's Decision

The Plumbing Place had two designers attend at Karston's place. I would think they would have the knowledge and expertise to know where the water supply pipes should go. Obviously, the pipes couldn't be installed in the two inside glass walls of the shower and would have to be installed with adequate insulation in an outside wall. With 18 years of experience it is absolutely incomprehensible to me how they could forget about the water pipes in their design for Karston.

For The Plumbing Place to demand a further $500 to correct its oversight is ludicrous.

The plaintiff, Karston, shall have his $3,500 deposit returned and he shall have his court costs. The counterclaim of the defendant, The Plumbing Place, is dismissed.

John Stillwell

vs.

Longshore Board of Education and Jack Snider, Principal of Long Beach Public School

Judge Adams's Decision

The Board and its principal, Jack Snider, had no right to refuse to provide John with the information he requested. They had no right to refuse information based on the temporary custody order in favour of the uncle, Earl. They had only to read the custody order to plainly see it expired in one year and, if they couldn't understand, they could have sought an interpretation from their legal counsel.

The Board and its principal shall forthwith provide the plaintiff, John Stillwell, with reports on his son and future reports as well. The Board shall pay Stillwell his court costs and his legal fees, which I set at $2,500.

ALAN AND EMILY CHERRY

VS.

QUICK AIR

JUDGE ADAMS'S DECISION

I accept the evidence of Alan and Emily Cherry that they were told to pack his nitroglycerine in his checked luggage.

It was my observation that the Cherrys, who indicated this was their first air trip, were confused as to the security requirements in regard to liquids, but the security people at the airport should have assisted the Cherrys, especially in view of their advanced ages.

Although the defendant airline representative gave evidence that no employee would ever tell the Cherrys they had to pack Alan's medicine, they did not see fit to call the check-in person to testify.

I find that the Cherrys were justified in returning home and they will have judgment against Quick Air for the price of their trip, namely $2,510, plus the cost of their taxi ride to Barrie in the amount of $160 and their court costs for this action, which I assess at $450.

James Snow

vs.

We Park — You Fly

Judge Adams's Decision

The defendant's attempt to avoid liability is absolutely ludicrous. If Snow had not left his keys in his car, it would be either sitting where he left it or would have been towed to the knowledge of the defendant and they would have known where it was.

The defendant's attempt to use the clause on the ticket denying responsibility will not let it off the hook either. This is a clear case of bailment for value and the company is responsible.

James Snow will have judgment for all his noted expenses and shall have his parking charges returned. In addition, he will have judgment for his inconvenience, which I assess at $500, and his court costs.

GRACE BECKER

VS.

BRITISH AMERICAN INSURANCE CO.

JUDGE ADAMS'S DECISION

Grace admitted she had the only keys. There was no evidence, as indicated by the police officer, of the car having been broken into.

The expert witness on steering columns gave critical evidence that the plaintiff did not dispute.

I accept the evidence of the expert witness and can only conclude that Grace, or someone hired by her, drove her limo to Kitchener to an area familiar to her and set her vehicle on fire. The fact, also, that she was having trouble selling the vehicle puts even more suspicion on her actions.

Grace's case is dismissed. The defendant insurance company, British American Insurance Co., will have its costs, including the cost of the expert witness, totalling $7,200.

Ralph Nizer

vs.

Long Range Transport Ltd.

Judge Adams's Decision

First, I have to decide if the plaintiff is entitled to his wages and whether he was justified in abandoning his rig. Second, I have to decide if the company was justified in refusing the fill-up requested by the plaintiff and if it should have its expenses in returning its transport.

The defendant, for whatever reason, did not see fit to call the driver sent to pick up the rig and bring it back to Hamilton and there was therefore no evidence that they did, in fact, return without refuelling.

I accept the evidence of the plaintiff that he was genuinely upset about running out of fuel. Notwithstanding the company's system for drivers to refuel and even if Nizer had ample fuel, I believe they could have made an exception and allowed him to refuel.

The defendant will have his wages as claimed, plus $20 per hour for his waiting time and his court costs. The defendant's claim is dismissed without costs.

SEE THRU WINDOWS INC.

VS.

JASON STOWKOWSKI

JUDGE ADAMS'S DECISION

The contract between the plaintiff and the defendant was a binding contract, there being an offer, an acceptance, and consideration of $8,500.

The company has no right to demand a further deposit and, as they were not prepared to proceed without it, the defendant is justified in terminating the contract.

The plaintiff's claim is dismissed and the defendant will have return of his deposit, plus his court costs, which I fix at $350.

CHARLES WILSON

VS.

SNELGRASS DEVELOPMENT LTD.

JUDGE ADAMS'S DECISION

While the advertising brochure was incorrect, I cannot find that it was in any way fraudulent. Wilson is getting what he viewed and, although the east limit is short of what was advertised, he is not getting a smaller lot.

It is also interesting that several lots to the east of lot 33 appear to have roughly the same depth as lot 33, namely 215 and 216 feet. This is clearly evident in Snelgrass's advertising brochure.

Wilson is in no worse position than he bargained for and has suffered no monetary loss.

The plaintiff's claim fails and is dismissed, but Wilson will have his court costs assessed at $315 because of the improper advertising, though unintentional, by Snelgrass.

Sandra Strong

vs.

Empire Discount Furniture

Judge Adams's Decision

Throughout the trial Empire's representatives gave questionable testimony and admitted that they could have been wrong about the material sample. Why they made such an issue of the matter is beyond this court. Sandra will have judgment for the $4,580 she paid, all the court costs, and a counsel fee of $500. Empire will have 15 days to pick up the furniture from Sandra's condo.

Jennifer Hurdle

vs.

Jeffrey Capriotti

Judge Adams's Decision

First of all, persons have a right to walk on a municipal sidewalk without interference from any source. The fact that Capriotti had a sign on the gate certainly indicates that persons should take care not to go near Tyler. There is no evidence that shows whether the gate was latched or open, but the fact is that Tyler came bounding out, while being yelled at the by defendant.

Whether Jennifer was afraid of dogs or paranoid about them is of no significance. She went on to the road to avoid Tyler and yet he continued to approach her and knock her down. Capriotti is responsible in law as the owner of Tyler and Jennifer will have judgment for her medical bills and court costs as well as $6,000 for her injuries.

Bulk Hay Ltd.

vs.

Gerald Nash

Judge Adams's Decision

There is some conflicting evidence as to whether the defendant notified the plaintiff to remove the hay. I accept the evidence of Nash that he did, in fact, notify Bulk Hay to remove the hay. I would say that he was not under any obligation to notify the plaintiff in any event. Nash said he agreed to have the hay remain on his property until the spring of 2002. I accept his evidence that a letter was sent on June 29, 2003.

I find that the hay was left by Bulk Hay at its own risk and its failure to remove the hay and the deterioration that resulted was its problem. I find that Nash's action in dumping the already ruined hay at the back of his farm to clean the driveway was prudent and reasonable.

The loss suffered by the plaintiff in not being able to export the hay to its New York mushroom grower was self-inflicted and the defendant is in no way responsible.

The plaintiff's case is dismissed. The defendant, Gerald Nash, shall have his costs, which are $115, and his counsel's fee, which I set at $900.

TIM AND LAURA O'GRADY

VS.

GEORGE AND SYLVIA WATERS

JUDGE ADAMS'S DECISION

The defendants cannot rely on "buyer beware." They knew that their pool was in bad shape. They knew that the pool had been condemned by the municipality. They should have known enough to drain the water heater, but appeared to ignore the potential problem of the freezing and cracking of the heat exchanger.

The purchasers were unable to check out the liner of the pool equipment on or before April 15 because of the cold weather and the snow.

The plaintiffs will be successful in their action. They will have judgment for $8,350, plus court costs and a counsel fee of $500.

SYLVIA HERON

VS.

OWEN SOUND CONCRETE DRIVEWAY PAVING LTD.

JUDGE ADAMS'S DECISION

I accept Sylvia Heron's evidence about the problem that, incidentally, the defendant does not deny. I accept her evidence that she did not put salt on the driveway. The evidence of Sam Biltmore about the quality of the concrete was straightforward and I accept as being correct.

This leaves one possible answer and that is that the paving was done incorrectly by Owen Sound Concrete Driveway Paving Ltd.

In regard to the matter of the six-month warranty, I find that this is totally unreasonable and that it is far too short a period, especially in the winter months.

Heron said she was unwilling to have the defendant redo the job as she has lost faith in its ability to do a good job.

The plaintiff shall have judgment for the cost of the driveway, namely $7,350 and costs.

Star Movers Ltd.

vs.

Stanley Baird

Judge Adams's Decision

It seems to me that Stanley Baird, throughout the whole affair, was the cause of his own problems. He agreed initially to have his dining room table crated. He didn't show up on time on moving day to let the movers in. He decided not to move into the Tindle Street house.

I find, as a fact, that he requested his furniture be put into storage and that he was aware of the cost. I also find that when he gave his cheque for $2,875 he knew he was going to put a stop payment on it. I agree with the plaintiff's contention that an estimate is only an estimate and not a binding contract.

There will be judgment for Star Movers Ltd. for $2,875, plus court costs, plus a counsel fee of $500.

JACK STARR

VS.

WHITE CONDOMINIUM CORPORATION

JUDGE ADAMS'S DECISION

Walters was absolutely correct in his submission that the problem was not that of the defendant, but that of the owner of condo 1710, although I make no finding in that regard as that party is not involved in this specific action.

The plaintiff's claim against White Condominium Corporation is dismissed with court costs to the defendant. This, of course, is without prejudice to the plaintiff to take action against any other party he sees fit.

BANK OF TORONTO

VS.

GARY SIMPSON

JUDGE ADAMS'S DECISION

Although Gary could be said to be morally responsible for this debt, he is not legally responsible. As the bank was unable to prove Gary signed as guarantor, they cannot collect from him.

The bank's only hope of collecting is to go after George's estate, but it appears it has exhausted that avenue.

The claim therefore against Gary Simpson is dismissed and the plaintiff will pay his court costs and $200 as an inconvenience fee.

SARAH SMART

VS.

VORTEX LTD.

JUDGE ADAMS'S DECISION

I thought it interesting that neither lawyer dwelt on the matter of Sarah being on probation for four months, although it was mentioned in the defendant's pleadings.

Probation aside, it certainly appears to me that Sarah's conduct and demeanour were not up to company standards. She was warned and given a chance and it appears she was defiant. Her conduct here today and the evidence of her dress at work indicates to me that she likes to march to her own drummer.

The plaintiff's case is dismissed. The defendant, having been put to considerable expense, shall have its court costs that I fix at $450 and a counsel fee of $450.

Venture Telephone Inc.

vs.

Josh Perry

Judge Adams's Decision

Perry's evidence was a little bit fuzzy. He couldn't precisely say what he told Venture when he attempted to cancel his arrangement with them.

He seemed to indicate that he didn't pay much attention to bills that came in and, in fact, admitted that he pitched any Venture bills in the garbage. It is also a bit peculiar that he didn't realize that his new service with his new supplier was considerably cheaper than with Venture.

I accept the evidence of Goodfellow, who had an accurate accounting of Perry's debt. I believe Perry through inadvertence or reckless abandon got himself into this unfortunate situation in which he now finds himself. His conduct is going to cost him what he owes.

There will be judgment to Venture Telephone Inc. for $4,373, plus court costs.

GERRY LISANTI

VS.

PEOPLE'S INSURANCE CO.

JUDGE ADAMS'S DECISION

I interpret the plaintiff's cancellation form sent on January 27 as meaning that the cancellation would be in the future, namely March 12. The words, "I no longer will be insuring with you," do not in my opinion mean, "I cancel now."

When we look at the case from the plaintiff's position, the question is: why would he cancel ahead of the expiry date of his policy? I don't think that was his intention.

The plaintiff will have judgment for $7,953, plus court costs.

MARIA SELFRIDGE

VS.

WEDDING TIME BANQUET HALL

JUDGE ADAMS'S DECISION

It appears that the court office has not yet received the trustee's notice of bankruptcy. If they had, it could have been put in my file and this matter could have been dwelt with in about two minutes instead of the two hours it took.

Unfortunately, Maria's claim cannot proceed in the court under the rules of the Bankruptcy Act.

Once someone makes an assignment in bankruptcy, all proceedings are stayed. This, however, does not prevent the claimant from filing a claim with the trustee in bankruptcy with the hope of receiving all or part of her money back.

The plaintiff's claim is therefore dismissed.

MARIO PESTRELLI

VS.

CONAIR INC.

JUDGE ADAMS'S DECISION

This is an interesting case. The loss of a passenger's luggage is, in fact, covered by the Warsaw Convention, but in this case I find that the luggage was not lost but merely misplaced causing a great deal of inconvenience and anxiety to the plaintiff.

I find that the Warsaw Convention, which regulates passenger losses, does not apply in this case.

For his suffering and inconvenience the plaintiff shall have judgment for $5,000, plus his court costs.

JANE ROSS

VS.

GORDON GREGORY

JUDGE ADAMS'S DECISION

I take judicial notice of the fact that many new homes have moisture problems because of the improved construction and insulation now being used. This is probably truer of homes such as Ross's, which appears to be a little more upscale than the usual run-of-the-mill, mass-produced subdivision homes.

The defendant, Gregory, testified he had no water problems and I accept his evidence.

The evidence of Short, the expert, was also believable and I accept his evidence.

The bottom line is that the plaintiff caused the moisture problem, which was the source of her action against the defendant, by turning off the hydro, thus disenabling the operation of the air exchanger system.

The plaintiff's action therefore fails and is dismissed with costs to the defendant. I set the defendant's expert's fees at $360, as billed by him, and all other costs will be on the usual scale.

CARMAN BISERI

VS.

JACK GEORGE

JUDGE ADAMS'S DECISION

The plaintiff's claim is totally without foundation. He entered into a lease for two years on terms he approved. That Eric Carmeli got a better deal as a result of a reduction in Jack George's insurance premium is none of the plaintiff's business. His claim, therefore, fails and he will pay the defendant's costs, which I fix at $650.

JANICE GOOD

VS.

QUICK LOAN INC.

JUDGE ADAMS'S DECISION

I have calculated the rate of interest the plaintiff was charged and, to put it quite frankly, it is usury without a doubt and borders on criminal. The Criminal Code provides for charges to be laid for excessive interest charges. While this court does not have any jurisdiction in criminal matters, it certainly can penalize persons for the usurious interest rates.

The plaintiff's claim for refund of the excessive interest shall be awarded. Because Janice still owes the defendant money, the interest will be set off against what she owes Quick Loan. Any excess owed by Janice will not be recovered by Quick Loan and Quick Loan will pay all of Janice's court costs.

Dorothy McKay

vs.

James Harrington, Carrying on Business as Wellington Stables

Judge Adams's Decision

First of all, I accept the evidence of both Dorothy McKay and Joyce Lattimer that there is an unwritten guarantee among horse dealers and their customers that if the purchaser is not satisfied a horse could be returned.

Second, I accept Dr. Sniderman's unequivocal and undisputed evidence that Jocko had a neurological disease that has no cure.

Third, I do not accept Harrington's evidence that the cause of the poor performance of Jocko at the Royal Winter Fair was because of his hernia operation. That evidence was unsubstantiated by medical evidence.

I think Harrington knew about Jocko's problem even if he didn't know about the seriousness of it.

The plaintiff shall have judgment for $6,800, but will return the horse to Harrington. McKay will also have her costs of this trial, including the examination and report from the veterinary college, which I understand cost her $2,163, and her counsel's fee of $1,300.

STAN JOHN

VS.

JACK STAR CLEANERS

JUDGE ADAMS'S DECISION

I accept the evidence of the plaintiff that he purchased the jacket about three weeks before he took it to the defendant. If the jacket's embroidery was damaged, why would Jack Star not bring it to John's attention and get him to sign a waiver or acknowledgement of the condition? I also find it difficult to accept the defendant's unsubstantiated lab report.

This jacket, from my own observation of it, was a really beautiful jacket and John's receipt proved that he paid $750.

Someone who takes in an item for work or service is a bailee and assumes responsibility for the care of that item while in his possession, unless appropriate waivers are signed.

I therefore find the defendant, Jack Star Cleaners, responsible for the damage of the plaintiff's jacket. The plaintiff shall have judgment for $750 plus court costs.

Timothy Sheerwood

vs.

John Grant, Carrying on Business as Grant's Parking

Judge Adams's Decision

The facts in this case are not in dispute. The car was left with Grant and was apparently stolen from his lot.

A person who takes the care and control of a vehicle for the purpose of repairing it or storing it or, as in this case providing a parking spot, is called a bailee and a bailee is responsible for the vehicle unless he very specifically indicates on the sign on his office and on the parking ticket that he assumes no responsibility for loss or damage.

Grant did not have such an endorsement on his rate sign, nor did his tickets indicate such. Grant's Parking is therefore responsible for the loss and Timothy Sheerwood shall have judgment for the sum claimed, namely $10,000, which includes the cost of his replacement vehicle and the rental charges. He will also have court costs.

Progress Hardwood Flooring Inc.

vs.

Charles and Eva Spanning

Judge Adams's Decision

Progress did not offer any expert evidence to dispute the evidence of Tom Lawson about the moisture content. There seemed to be no dispute that the cherry hardwood did, in fact, have a high moisture content. It also appears that, even after four or so months with the heat on in the Spannings' house, the problem remained. I do take judicial notice of the fact (the judge already knows) that an air exchanger gets rid of the normal moisture build up in a house.

I can only come to the conclusion that the cherry hardwood supplied by Progress was extremely high in moisture content and had not been properly dried.

I accept the evidence of Tom Lawson regarding the moisture content and his solution to the problem, namely replacing the hardwood flooring.

The plaintiff's case is therefore dismissed and the defendants will have judgment for $3,150, plus their court costs and their counsel, which I set at $450.

JOHN AND SARAH SHAPIRO

VS.

AIRPORT MANAGEMENT INC.

JUDGE ADAMS'S DECISION

As the defendant did not choose to call the security employee to testify, I have to accept the evidence of Sarah that the employee knocked the computer off the table resulting in the damage claimed.

If there is, in fact, a sign advising travellers that they are responsible for their possessions, I cannot interpret that as meaning the defendant can be negligent in the handling of items it insists be put through the X-ray process.

I accept the evidence of John Shapiro in regard to the pricing of the new computer. John Shapiro will have judgment for $1,218 and his court costs. As Sarah Shapiro had no ownership in the computer, it was not necessary for her to be a plaintiff and her claim is dismissed.

APARTMENT RENTALS INC.

VS.

DIANE SAWYER

JUDGE ADAMS'S DECISION

Diane is responsible for the rent until the sheriff obtained possession of the apartment for the plaintiff. She is also responsible for the court costs paid to the court that the sheriff set at $800. She is also responsible for the clear out of the apartment and a reasonable amount for decorating, which I set at $600. I accept the evidence of the landlord about the hole in the floor and the larger hydro bills he received and I set that amount at $320. In all, the plaintiff shall have judgment for $7,570, plus the costs of this action and the plaintiff's lawyer's counsel fee, which I set at $550.

ARNOLD WHITNEY

VS.

VALLEY VIEW FARMS INC.

JUDGE ADAMS'S DECISION

The plaintiff in the action obviously did not know of a somewhat peculiar law in this jurisdiction and I will paraphrase that law for him as follows: "every person who, being the owner or having the care, custody or control of horses, cattle, swine, sheep or goats, suffers or permits them or any of them to run at large within the limits of the highway, is guilty of an offence punishable on summary conviction," and these are the operative words, "this provision does not create any civil liability on the part of the owner of an animal for damage caused to the property of others as a result of the animal running at large within the limits of the highway." This provision can be found in the Public Transportation and Highway Improvement Act.

I know this seems unfair to the plaintiff, but I can only administer and interpret the law as it is written by our legislators. The plaintiff's claim is therefore dismissed. There will be no cost awarded to either party.

John Grey

vs.

Fred Grey

Judge Adams's Decision

When I asked both Fred and John why they didn't ask their township for fence viewers to resolve this dispute, they both said they were unaware of the existence of such a remedy. During the trial, I explained to them that most townships will appoint fence viewers under the Line Fence Act to resolve line fence disputes.

Not having availed themselves of the Line Fence Act provisions, the decision now rests with me. It is unfortunate that Fred has taken a stubborn stance on this whole matter. If he decided to go into the milk business, then he had an obligation to prevent his cows from wandering onto John's property or the property of anyone else.

What the fence viewers would do if they had been called in is exactly what I am going to do. Each party is responsible for installing and maintaining a portion of a property line fence. That portion is exactly one-half.

As Fred installed 1,000 feet of fence at a cost of $5,000, John is responsible for one-half the cost, being $2,500. Fred is responsible for the cost and maintenance of 1,200 feet of the five-wire fence that John installed, in addition to the cost and maintenance of the 1,000 feet he put in, in other words, the front 2,200 feet of five-wire fence.

John is responsible for the rear 2,200 feet of the five-wire fence he installed. I accept John's evidence that his crop loss because of Fred's cows was $1,080.

I must now work out the financial cost and responsibility for the installation of the fences.

Fred paid $5,000 and John paid $7,560 in total for the fences they erected. These two sums total $12,560. Fred and John should each pay one-half this total or $6,280.

Of the $6,280 Fred owes, he paid $5,000, leaving a balance owing by him of $1,280. John paid $7,560 for his fence, although he actually owes only $6,280, so he must be reimbursed by Fred by $1,280.

John Grey shall have judgment for $1,280 plus the $1,080 for crop damage. John will also receive his costs of this action, which I am fixing at $550.

SANDRA AND GEORGE SILTON

VS.

MARIA JACOBSON

JUDGE ADAMS'S DECISION

As I indicated the evidence of the parties is conflicting. The defendant did admit switching the refrigerator, which certainly was interesting. I do accept the Silton's evidence that all the appliances had been replaced with inferior quality ones.

There will be judgment to the plaintiffs for $4,600, plus court costs and a counsel fee for their lawyer for $550.

Jack's Garage Inc.

vs.

Ralph Menzie

Judge Adams's Decision

I accept the evidence of Ralph Menzie that his transmission leaked after he got his vehicle back from Jack's Garage.

Jack's attitude about having nothing further to do with Menzie seems to be inappropriate in view of the evidence that there was, in fact, a problem with his work. Jack's did not call any evidence to dispute the evidence of Larry Schmidt, which was credible and believable.

The plaintiff's claim is dismissed.

In regard to the defendant's counterclaim, Menzie should certainly not be compensated for the full amount of his claim, otherwise he would have received a new transmission at no cost. He was prepared to pay Jack's $2,383, but ended up paying Fast Transmissions $2,830. He will, therefore, receive judgment for $447, being the extra he had to pay Fast Transmissions. Menzie will also receive his costs of the counterclaim.

ROBERT HOWARD

VS.

WE PARK — YOU FLY

JUDGE ADAMS'S DECISION

I am prepared to accept the evidence of Robert Howard that there was no damage when he left his car. I am also prepared to accept the evidence of Jack Smart, the mechanic from Lexus, that there was no possible way the car could have rolled down the slope once the engine was shut off.

I find therefore that Jeffrey White, the defendant's employee who parked the car, recklessly drove the car into the fence.

The second point to be considered is whether the defendant's waiver on the ticket was sufficient to allow the defendant to successfully deny liability.

I find the defendant to be grossly negligent in the parking of the car. As a bailee for value the defendant might be able to avoid liability in certain cases, but not where there has been gross negligence.

I give judgment to the plaintiff for $2,715, plus costs and a counsel fee of $650.

Gordon Snelgrove

vs.

Union Insurance Co.

Judge Adams's Decision

A transfer of title of a motor vehicle from an individual to a corporation owned solely by the individual for business convenience without any change in beneficial ownership is not a change in the insurable interest of the individual within the Insurance Act.

The plaintiff will therefore have judgment for $8,550, plus court costs.

James Beer

vs.

Northern Railway Co.

Judge Adams's Decision

I think the defendant's liability, if any, is that of a gratuitous bailee and the law is quite clear that a gratuitous bailee is only responsible for "gross negligence." Higher courts have said that if "no one can fairly say that the means employed for the protection of property were not such as any reasonable man might properly have considered amply sufficient" a gratuitous bailee could not be held liable.

The defendant's witness about the inspection of the boiler was reasonable and I accept that evidence.

I find that the explosion was not due to the negligence of the defendant and certainly there is no indication that there was gross negligence.

The plaintiff's case is therefore dismissed.

LAWRENCE AITKEN

VS.

QUICK REPAIR AND TOWING INC.

JUDGE ADAMS'S DECISION

The plaintiff was put in the position by the defendant that if he didn't pay, additional charges would accumulate on the already hefty bill. He was also put in the position that he needed his vehicle repaired as soon as possible so he could get to work.

The defendant did not have an independent witness to back up its charges, whereas Aitken had the evidence of George Still of A & B Towing and Storage. I accept the evidence of Still, which seemed to be truthful and reasonable.

The plaintiff shall therefore have his money returned, less what he agreed in this court to pay. Judgment is awarded to the plaintiff for $430, plus his court costs.

GORDON BOE

VS.

FIRE EQUIPMENT INC.

JUDGE ADAMS'S DECISION

For an employer to terminate an employee for just cause, they need to have warned the employee about his inappropriate conduct and document the warnings. An employee of almost 10 years must be advised of any problems and requested to correct them.

An arbitrary decision to dismiss an employee who merely requested clarification of his position is unjustified and certainly does not warrant dismissal for cause.

The plaintiff shall have judgment for $10,000, plus his court costs and a counsel fee of $800.

James Carswell

vs.

King Hotel Inc.

Judge Adams's Decision

There is no dispute that Carswell was badly burned in the shower stall of his room at the defendant's hotel.

The defendant has not satisfied me that the plaintiff must seek compensation in Nova Scotia. The Ontario doctor and Ontario hospital that looked after his injury told him that, because he was from another province, he was not covered in Ontario. I think it is common practice for people travelling outside their own province or, country to obtain out-of-province insurance coverage. Carswell, apparently, had no such insurance, so he was left with the only remaining remedy and that was to sue the hotel.

King Hotel cannot escape liability by saying that Oscar Schmidt was a contract employee. He might not have been an employee in the usual sense, receiving a fixed salary or hourly wage and benefits, but he was working for the hotel and was under the direction of the hotel management. If Schmidt was doing his job poorly, he could have been terminated by the hotel. The defendant is responsible for what happened to Carswell and there will be judgment to him for $765 for the hospital and $1,000 for his pain and suffering, plus an allowance for inconvenience, which I set at $300.

Gordon Seeborn

vs.

Northern Blasting Inc.

Judge Adams's Decision

I agree with the counsel for the defendant that there is no evidence from which this court can conclude any cracks were caused by this particular blast on May 3. The plaintiff's witness, Charles Acorn, pointed out that there were several other areas of the wall that had been patched by concrete. This leads me to think that the cracks the plaintiff is complaining about may have occurred by a settling of the house which is a common occurrence.

The plaintiff's case is dismissed for lack of proof. The plaintiff will be responsible for the defendant's costs, which I set at $450.

Carol Jamieson

vs.

North West Insurance Co.

Judge Adams's Decision

It appears to be abundantly clear that Small was using the old house for the illegal purpose of growing marijuana. It is also clear that the hydro meter was by-passed. It is common knowledge that this type of activity requires a considerable use of hydro. As the plaintiff has testified that her hydro bills were nothing out of the ordinary, I accept her evidence. I find that she could not have known that anything unusual was happening in her old house.

The defendant cannot refuse to pay if it cannot prove the plaintiff had knowledge of the illegal activity and it has not done so. The plaintiff has satisfied me on the evidence that her claim is legitimate and she will have judgment for her claim in full, as well as her costs, which I set at $700.

George Downey

vs.

Arthur Ross

Judge Adams's Decision

In this case the facts are not in dispute. The plaintiff left 2,000 bushels of corn in a bin with the permission of Angus Reid hoping to get a better price the following year. It remained in the bin after Reid had sold the farm to Ross. Ross sold the corn and received $7,500 from Harvey Potter who ran the local grain elevator.

The defence is that the plaintiff had abandoned the corn and no longer had title to it. The law on conversion is quite clear and can be stated as thus:

> At common law one's duty to one's neighbour who is the owner, or entitled to possession of any goods, is to refrain from doing any voluntary act in relation to his good which is a usurpation of his proprietary or possessory rights in them, it matters not that the doer of the act of usurpation did not know, and could not by the exercise of any reasonable care have known of his neighbour's interest in the goods. The duty is absolute and he acts at his peril.

It does not matter that the defendant did not know that the plaintiff had an interest in the goods. Since the defendant failed to enquire into the ownership of the corn, he was guilty of conversion unless he could show abandonment. The onus of proving abandonment is on the party alleging it and not on the owner. In this case the defendant has not proved abandonment. There will be judgment to the plaintiff for $7,500, plus his court costs, which I fix at $325.

Jerry Young, Legal Representative of Andy Young and Jerry Young in His Personal Capacity

vs.

Charles Snider and Simcoe Hurricanes AAA Peewee Hockey Club and Simcoe Hurricanes Hockey Association

Judge Adams's Decision

First of all let me say that, as the father of three hockey playing boys, I know something about hockey and have observed much of the conduct of players and parents, and a great deal of it is, to say the least, unpleasant. However, I am not saying that I have prejudged this case, but only that I take judicial notice of what happens in minor hockey.

I accept the evidence of Coach Snider as to the manner in which he was treated by Andy and Jerry Young. The evidence indicated that Coach Snider was a qualified and experienced coach. The evidence also indicates that Jerry Young was a disturber in the dressing room and as a spectator in the arena. I find as a fact that Snider had good cause to eject him from the dressing room. The coach must have control of his hockey team and must be able at this competitive level to decide who plays or doesn't play at any particular game.

I find that Charles Snider acted as a reasonable coach at all levels and do not find that Andy was let go because of his father, but because of his lack of skill and effort on the ice.

There will be no order for reinstatement of Andy and the plaintiff's case is dismissed. The defendants will have their costs, which I assess at $315, and a counsel fee of $700.

Ravi and Norida Salib

vs.

Kapoor Sandeen

Judge Adams's Decision

The parties having come to a settlement my job is greatly simplified. However, in order to see that the defendant sticks to his promise, I do award judgment to the plaintiffs for $3,500 to be paid within 10 days, and I further order that the defendant hand over to the plaintiffs the 785 photos without any marking on them and this is to be done within the next 10 days as well.

If the defendant fails to abide by this judgment, the parties will be summoned to appear before me at which time I will give a different judgment than this one today.

Larson August

vs.

Carl James, Carrying on Business as Carl's Dry Cleaning

Judge Adams's Decision

There is an abundance of law that clearly indicates that a mere waiver of the kind on the order form is not sufficient to enable the defendant to deny payment. The law is very clear that a waiver must be clearly seen and pointed out to the customer. James admitted that he had not brought the waiver to the attention of August. Therefore, I hold that the waiver does not let James "off the hook." The second matter to consider is whether this was an "Act of God" or a fire so suspicious that the insurance company would not pay. There was no evidence produced by the plaintiff that charges had been laid or, in fact, the defendant had been prosecuted as a result of the suspicious fire. I cannot assume that, just because the insurance company had decided the fire was suspicious, it was, in fact, suspicious, or that the defendant was responsible. If the defendant had been charged with arson and convicted, I might have taken a different view of the matter. In my opinion the plaintiff has failed to prove his case based on a balance of probabilities and his action fails. The defendant shall have his costs, which I fix at $300.

Dr. Joseph Ryan

vs.

Clare Innes

Judge Adams's Decision

This has been a long case with conflicting evidence. It appears to me that the defendant, Innes, wanted his aching tooth fixed and paid a deposit of $400 to have the work done. I accept the evidence of Dr. Ryan that Innes agreed to pay the balance over a two-month period. I also accept the evidence of Dr. George Bower and particularly that of Dr. Sally Wrightman whose evidence stands uncontradicted by Innes.

Dr. Ryan has proved his case and Innes has in no way shaken the evidence of the plaintiff or his witnesses. Usually I do not make comments in regard to a person's evidence or demeanour, but in this case I suggest that Innes has been far from truthful and that he tried to use the kindness of Dr. Ryan to avoid paying the account.

There will be judgment for Dr. Ryan and the claim of Clare Innes for $400 will be dismissed. Innes will also pay Dr. Ryan's court costs plus an allowance of $600 to cover his attendance and that of Emily Parrotski. If Dr. Ryan is out of pocket to the other two dentists for their affidavit evidence, the cost of that, as determined by the court clerk, will be added to the award to Dr. Ryan.

ANDREW AND CHRISTINE BARKLY

VS.

VACATIONS IN THE SUN LTD.

JUDGE ADAMS'S DECISION

I accept the evidence of the plaintiffs. These types of disastrous holidays are happening all too frequently and in this case it certainly appears that the brochure put out by the defendant was not only misleading, but blatantly untrue. People shouldn't have to put up with this kind of false advertising, nor should they have to absorb the cost of getting themselves out of the mess.

There will be judgment to the plaintiffs for $4,235.13.

I will now address the matter of costs. Davis has indicated that an offer of settlement was served on the plaintiffs and filed in the court office. I will now open the sealed envelope to determine the amount of the offer. The parties should know, as I'm sure Davis knows, that, if the judgment exceeds the offer, all costs will be double at the discretion of this court.

The offer of settlement filed is in the amount of $3,000. As this amount is less than my judgment, the plaintiffs' costs being court costs of $135, and an allowance for inconvenience of $400 totalling $535 will be doubled to $1,070 payable by the defendant.

Fred Jones, Carrying on Business as Jones Butcher Shop,

VS.

Jason McKay

Judge Adams's Decision

There is no dispute that this was an oral contract and there is no dispute that Jones suffered a loss as a result of the loss of the McKay hogs. How much that loss is, is a question that has to be answered. Jones's claim is based on what he believes will be his loss over the next two years. I do not believe that that loss can be pinpointed exactly. The price of hogs might decrease and the number of orders Jones gets may decrease. There was no evidence presented to me that Jones had to take all 50 hogs each year. I find that there was no contract that was binding on either party. Any business relationship that existed between the parties came to an end when the fire destroyed the subject matter of the relationship. Had there been a written contract specifically outlining the rights and obligation of the parties, I might have found differently, but in this case action I cannot find for the plaintiff and his case is dismissed. There will be no costs to either party.

MARY ELIZABETH CLARK

VS.

JACK JORDAN, CARRYING ON BUSINESS AS JORDAN GOLDEN RETRIEVER KENNELS

JUDGE ADAMS'S DECISION

This is not an unusual case. I think that during my years on the bench I have run into similar situations a number of times. I even had a case where a horse that was not sound was returned and the defendant horse dealer was obliged to return the purchaser's money.

I am not in any way letting my previous decision influence what I am saying here.

This court is a court of equity as well as law. I find it difficult to say that in law Jordan is obliged to take back Fred and refund Clark's money, but in equity it seems to me that this type of transaction should not only appear to be fair but should on all fours be fair. Jordan is in the business of breeding and selling golden retrievers to the public and I think the public has a right to expect that a dog purchased from a qualified and certified breeder will be sound and free of any problems. Twelve hundred dollars is a lot to pay for a dog with problems.

There will be judgment to the plaintiff for $1,200 and court costs of $400. The plaintiff will return Fred to the defendant on payment of the $1,200 and costs.

Janice Simpson

vs.

Caledon Hills Rentals Inc., and Caledon Hills Rentals Inc. vs. George Nash and Audrey Porter

Judge Adams's Decision

First, I find there is no course of action against George Nash and the action against him is dismissed. As Nash did not defend and has not incurred any costs that I have been made aware of, there is no order for payment to him.

In regard to Janice Simpson's claim, it certainly does appear that she was inconvenienced and put to some expense in regard to the truck rental. She indicated that she was able to store her belongings for free in a friend's garage. Her cost of the truck rental was $265.

That leaves the question of liability or in other words who, if anybody, is to blame? Audrey Porter, the superintendent, seems to be the person who created the problem by not reading correctly and communicating to Caledon Hills Rentals Inc. the notice to vacate given by George Nash. Having said that, it is quite evident that Porter was an employee or agent of Caledon Hills. No evidence was introduced by Caledon Hills or Porter as to what the relationship was, but I assume that Caledon Hills compensated her in some way for looking after the apartments or, at least, looking after the renting of the apartment.

Ultimately, Caledon Hills Rentals is responsible for its employee's or agent's actions. I find that, on the evidence I have heard, Porter created the problem, which became Caledon's problem.

I find Caledon Hills Rentals Inc. responsible for any loss suffered by Janice Simpson and I assess her damage at $265 for the truck rental and $300 for her inconvenience and court costs. As she has already been paid $400 by Caledon that leaves a balance owing by Caledon of $165.

Regarding Caledon's claim against Porter, I find that Porter was negligent in the handling of this whole matter and should compensate Caledon for its expenses, which are $565. There will, therefore, be judgment for Caledon Hills Rentals Inc. against Audrey Porter for $565, which is inclusive of costs.

CLARE SNEDDON

VS.

GEORGE ANDERSON

JUDGE ADAMS'S DECISION

This is an interesting case in which the defendant, George Anderson, was unwilling to talk about a settlement and was quite adamant that his position was correct and the logger he hired was at fault. I would point out that Sneddon was not a party to the contract between George Anderson and the logger. I accept the plaintiff's evidence in regard to the survey, which clearly shows the lot line, and I also accept the evidence of Geoff Wozniak, the arborist, which was not disputed by the defendant.

If the defendant wanted the blame to be placed with the logger, he could have added him as a third party or party defendant to these proceedings. In fact he may still wish to pursue an action against the logger with whom there is probably privity of contract.

I find that the defendant is responsible for the cutting down of the plaintiff's trees. Had the plaintiff, as part of his action sued for more than just the economic loss he suffered, that is to say for some loss for aesthetics, I might have awarded something more, but as he didn't I do not have to deal with that possible aspect of the case.

Clare Sneddon will have judgment for $8,500, plus

court costs, which I set at $700, plus $1,600 for the survey and the arborist's bill of $825.

LINDA SNELGROVE

VS

CARMAN FREDERICO

JUDGE ADAMS'S DECISION

I find as a fact that the plaintiff did waive her right to have an inspection done before closing. I also find that the plaintiff did not supply any evidence to convince me that the basement refrigerator was working. I accept the defendant's evidence that the refrigerator was an old one that had not worked for years.

I also find, as a fact, the defendant did take a picture of the fence on April 2 and on examining the photo, it clearly shows that the one section of the fence was falling over. It looks to me from the photo that it was on an angle of about 30 to 35 degrees.

In summary the plaintiff has failed to prove her case and it will be dismissed.

The plaintiff will pay the defendant's court costs of $135 and the defendant's counsel fee, which I set at $650.

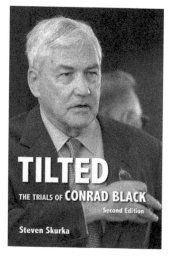

Tilted
The Trials of Conrad Black
Second Edition
by Steven Skurka
978-1-55488-934-1
$26.99

As the only Canadian writer to attend the trials of Conrad Black from start to finish, lawyer Steven Skurka delivers a thorough, in-depth account of the controversial businessman's legal difficulties. In this brand-new edition, Skurka offers updated analysis, insights, and personal anecdotes to present the clearest picture of the trials to date, featuring interviews with key members of the prosecution and defence, as well as with Black himself.

Under Arrest
Canadian Laws You Won't Believe
by Bob Tarantino
978-1-55002-703-7
$24.99

Did you know that Canada's Criminal Code still has provisions outlawing the practice of witchcraft and "crafty sciences"? Or that blasphemy is a crime in Canada?

Lawyer and author Bob Tarantino takes readers on an entertaining and informative romp through Canada's legal labyrinths in a book that spotlights the country's past and present strange-but-true laws and legal history. He examines odd statutes and arcane jurisprudence across the spectrum of Canadian endeavours, from war and religion to sex and culture to politics and business.

Justice Miscarried
Inside Wrongful Convictions in Canada
by Hélèna Katz
978-1-55488-874-0
$24.99

We may no longer legally enforce or advocate capital punishment in Canada, but *Justice Miscarried* proves that life can still be taken away from those who are wrongly convicted. Behind the proud facade of Canada's criminal justice system lie the shattered lives of the people unjustly caught within its web. This book tells the heart-wrenching stories of 12 innocent Canadians who were wrongly convicted and the errors in the nation's justice system that changed their lives forever.

Available at your favourite bookseller.

 **DUNDURN**
www.dundurn.com

What did you think of this book?
Visit *www.dundurn.com* for reviews, videos, updates,
and more!